Telling it like it was

Dent, Sedbergh and district in living memory

Volume 1

Telling it like it was

Dent, Sedbergh and district in living memory
Volume 1

ANTHEA BOULTON
and VERONICA WHYMANT
Illustrations by Pip Hall

Dales Historical Monographs
for Dent & Sedbergh Oral History Society

Published in 2015 by
Dales Historical Monographs, Hobsons Farm, Cowgill, Dent, Sedbergh,
Cumbria LA10 5RF
for Dent & Sedbergh Oral History Society
ISBN 978-0-9511578-8-6
©Dent & Sedbergh Oral History Society
Printed by Stramongate Press, Kendal, Cumbria.

Anthea Boulton studied English at Exeter University and joined Granada Television in 1964, writing local news stories, drama, and storylines for Coronation Street. After starting a family she freelanced for Radio Lancashire, writing and presenting a variety of programmes including documentaries based on local history. She was awarded a diploma in regional studies by Lancaster University, and served as a JP for twenty five years, first in Darwen, Lancashire, then on the Kendal Bench. In 1972 she and her husband David bought Hobsons Farm in Cowgill, Dentdale, and moved there permanently in 1991. They have two daughters and three grandsons. antheaboulton@btinternet.com

Veronica Whymant graduated in 2006 from the University of St. Andrews with an MA Honours degree in History and thereafter an MSc from Glasgow University in Information Management and Preservation. Since graduation she has been involved in numerous projects including work in Sedbergh School's archive department. Oral history is a field in which she would like to specialise further and she is currently involved with the oral archive of the St. Andrews Preservation Trust Museum, Fife. veronica.whymant@gmail.com

Pip Hall runs a lettering studio in Dentdale, where she carves inscriptions for commemoration and celebration, house signs and garden features, as well as carrying out public art commissions, and exhibiting. Pip's work also includes lettering and illustration for books, and for interiors, such as floors and walls. She runs short courses in lettercarving, and occasionally takes on apprentice-training with support from the Lettering and Commemorative Arts Trust at Snape Maltings, Suffolk. www.piphall.co.uk

Contents

Introduction
Acknowledgments
Introducing our contributors

Chapter 1 Childhood 1
   Freedom! 2
   Learner drivers 5
   Hunting and fishing 6
   Working for pocket money 8
   Learning skills at home... 9
   ...and on the farm 9
   Help in the home 11
   Family life – and death 12
   Entertainments and treats 13
   Christmas 15

Chapter 2 Schooldays 17
   Getting there 18
   Time out 21
   Makin' us use our brains' 22
   Discipline 27
   'Tig...skipping...marbles...hopscotch' 29
   No school dinners! 31

Chapter 3 Land and labour *33*
    Farm sizes and types *34*
    The workforce *38*
    Walling *41*
    Hiring fairs *42*

Chapter 4 Cattle *45*
    Types of herds *46*
    Milking and milk rounds *47*
    Cows to the customers *49*
    Butter and cheese *50*
    Milk collection and the Marketing Board *52*
    Modernisation – and decline *53*
    Beef rearing *55*
    Marketing, auction marts and 'luck' *56*
    Slaughtering *59*

Chapter 5 Sheep *61*
    Heafs *62*
    Breeds *62*
    Lambing *63*
    Washing, castrating, salving *64*
    Gathering, clipping, dipping *64*
    Sales *67*
    Yan, tan, tethera *68*
    One man and his dog *69*
    Subsidies *69*

Chapter 6 Pigs, poultry and game *71*
    The piggeries *72*
    The family pig *72*
    From pig to pork *74*
    Sharing *76*
    Rituals and superstitions *77*
    Dual occupation *78*

    Poultry and eggs *78*
    Knitting for game *80*

Chapter 7 Haytime *83*
    A serious business *84*
    Scythes *84*
    Rakes and sledges *85*
    Mowing, scaling, leading *87*
    And then there were tractors *91*
    Plats, pikes, cocks and kemmins *94*
    Dialect terms *94*
    Stacking the moo *96*
    When the sun wouldn't shine *98*
    Haytime refreshments *98*
    Helping the neighbours *100*

Chapter 8 Women's work *101*
    On the farm *102*
    Household chores *103*
    Wash days and smoothing irons *104*
    Feeding the family *105*
    Rug-making, sewing and knitting *107*
    Earning a living from home *108*
    Going out to work *109*
    Women's Institute *111*

Chapter 9 Hearth and home *113*
    Traditional houses *114*
    Baths and lavatories *118*
    Water supplies *119*
    Heating the home: peat and coal *121*
    Lamps and candle light *122*
    Gas *123*
    Electricity *124*
    Wartime prefabs *126*

- Social housing ... 127
- Sheltered housing ... 128
- Offcomers – the new property owners ... 129

Chapter 10 Love and friendship ... 131
- Courting ... 132
- Marriage and honeymoon ... 133
- When it went wrong ... 136
- Looking after each other ... 136
- All sorts ... 140

Chapter 11 Church and chapel ... 143
- Church ... 144
- Chapel ... 149
- Sunday school ... 153
- Closures ... 155
- Cradle and grave ... 157

Chapter 12 Fun and games ... 161
- Dancing ... 162
- Entertaining ourselves ... 164
- All the fun of the fair ... 168

Introduction

In 1994 a group of us set up the Dent Oral History Project, later expanded to the Dent and Sedbergh Oral History Society, with the aim of recording the memories of our neighbours in the local community. We chose Farfield Mill for our first topic, then widened our researches to take in recollections of Dentdale, the Sedbergh area, Howgill and Garsdale. Our overall purpose has been to explore how life here has changed within living memory.

Our project does not claim to be a comprehensive survey, which would have been beyond our resources. However, we have tried to build a representative archive. We invited contributions from farmers and housewives, shopkeepers and trades folk, teachers, builders and businessmen, craftspeople and clerics in our attempt to cover as many aspects of dales life as possible. We were delighted by the response. People asked us into their homes and generously shared with us their life stories, each one special in its own way. We are grateful to our interviewees for signing release forms which allowed their accounts to be made publicly available. This has ensured that these memories of a lost way of life will be preserved for future generations, not only in this book but in our archive.

In exploring the subject of change we decided to concentrate on those whose memories go back the furthest. Our oldest contributor was born in 1905 and several others grew up during the days of the First World War. We have many recollections of the interwar years and of life in the 1940s and '50s. The excerpts in this book are not given in chronological order, and since many readers may want to dip in and out we have given the interviewee's year of birth after each extract as an indication of the period being spoken of.

The resulting archive is a treasure trove of first-hand recollections that bring to light the character, and characters, of these dales. Time and again, describing life before the Second World War, our interviewees tell us 'it was different altogether, a different world'. These were days before the consumer society and social security, when families and neighbours relied on each other for support and the area tended to operate its own market economy. Incomes were generally low and many families experienced hard times, especially during the agricultural depression of the 1930s. People benefited, however, from a strong sense of community. Few folk travelled much outside their own locality and many stressed how social life in their young day was centred on the local church or chapel.

Growing mechanisation was a major cause of change in this period. Our interviewees remember the days when almost every job on the farm was done by hand and horse, and tell how tractors transformed their lives when they began to come into general use in the 1950s. The increasing number of motor vehicles made travelling and moving goods around so much easier than relying on a horse and cart.

The arrival of mains electricity was another development which brought enormous benefits. Aids such as milking machines and poultry incubators improved efficiency on the farm. Electric lights replaced dim candles and smoking oil lamps and lengthened the short winter days. In the home many respondents tell us how their lives were wonderfully improved by the new electrical appliances. Fridges helped keep their food fresh, vacuum cleaners and electric irons gave them better results with less effort, and washing machines meant they no longer had to slave all day over the old dolly tub.

It is not the purpose of this book to recount facts and figures. They can be found in the written record. Oral history is something else: it's about people telling their own stories in their own words. Inevitably the question arises: how far can we trust the accuracy of peoples' memories? Details tend to fade, especially as we get older, and memories can be selective, particularly when recounting our tales to other people, but this in no way diminishes their value. What comes over above all in these recordings is the lived experience: how it felt to be leading hay with a frisky horse through a narrow gate, or to hear the squeal of your slaughtered pig and then labour over hams and sausages and pig foot pie. Oral history allows us to become privileged onlookers as people go about their daily lives.

Our project would not have been possible without the input of a team of talented and dedicated helpers past and present, gratefully acknowledged below. With nearly a hundred recordings to draw from, organising material for this book was a daunting prospect and I could not have done it alone. So the arrival of Veronica Whymant in Sedbergh in 2009 was an amazing stroke of luck. Veronica already had a history degree plus a further degree in archiving, and came to work as a volunteer with Sedbergh School's archive department. It was Elspeth Griffiths who suggested that she might be interested in our oral history work. Veronica has been an invaluable member of our team ever since. She has become expert in all aspects of the project, working methodically through the archive, organising it into subjects and selecting appropriate extracts. It was obvious from the start that her contribution could only be adequately acknowledged by crediting her as co-author of the book.

My own interest in oral history grew from my experience in the media. After working at Granada TV as a reporter, dramatist and storyline writer for Coronation Street I moved over to radio and interviewed and wrote for BBC Radio Lancashire. My husband David brought his skills as both writer and newspaper and TV editor to the considerable job of editing this book, and we have benefited from the advice of another professional, Dr. Elizabeth Roberts, Lancashire University lecturer and acknowledged authority on oral history, who has acted as our consultant throughout. We were delighted when nationally renowned Cowgill-based artist Pip Hall offered to illustrate the book with her beautiful linocuts.

Recording an interview is only the first step in a long process. Next it has to be transcribed and, since most interviews are around ninety minutes long, this is a time-consuming business. Our transcribers are faced with the difficult job of recording the local dialect and, since transcribing is an art, not a science, differences have inevitably arisen in the way they've tackled this. Some have followed every subtle speech sound, others have written the speech in a more standard form. All have noted down the hesitations and repetitions which we all use in everyday speech but, while these remain in the full transcripts, we have felt at liberty to limit them in the extracts, and occasionally to tighten up the syntax. We have balanced the need to reflect the personality and dialect of the person being interviewed with the need to make their words accessible to the general reader. Too little portrayal of dialect and speech rhythms robs an interviewee of his or her voice, too much may make reading wearisome and we hope we have struck a reasonable balance.

This is the first of two volumes to be based on the archive. In this book we move from childhood and school days to the subject of work, on the farm and in the home. We hear about family life, church life and the entertainments folk enjoyed. The second volume will include descriptions of shops and shopping, work in the mills and other industries, transport, and accounts of local peoples' experiences during the Second World War.

The full archive contains many more fascinating stories than we are able to include in our two volumes and if you would like to hear the recordings and read the transcripts they can be easily accessed on our computer in the room run by the Sedbergh and District History Society at the Community Offices, 72 Main Street, Sedbergh.

The social developments revealed in these pages are not peculiar to the Dent, Sedbergh and Garsdale area. In the twentieth century people all over Britain lived through massive change. In some respects, though, our area can claim to be special. The relative remoteness of its location has meant that change has come more slowly, and the effects of this remoteness have rippled through the centuries. It has encouraged a hard-working, self sufficient community and a traditional way of life which lives on in peoples' memories. We hope this book will help to preserve a record for the years to come.

Anthea Boulton

Chair, Dent and Sedbergh Oral History Society

May 2015

Acknowledgments

Our oral history project could not have been carried out without the support of local community organisations and dedicated individuals. At the start of the project we received generous financial assistance from the Sedbergh and District History Society, Farfield Mill, the Dent and Sedbergh Parish Councils, and Colin Barnett. The Kendal Oral History Society gave us valuable advice and encouragement. More recently, grants earmarked to help cover the costs of producing this book have been gratefully received from the Sedbergh and District Community Fund, South Lakeland District Councillor Ian McPherson's community fund, and Dent Parish Council.

Key to the success of the project has been the team who joined Anthea Boulton as interviewers. Valuable early work was done by Betty Harper, Isobel Stacey, Audrey Douglas, Bryan Hinton and Christine Wood. Currently, interviews in the Sedbergh area are conducted by Julie Leigh, who honed her interviewing skills while working as a secondary school teacher. Dilys Evans interviews in the Garsdale area with the help of Elizabeth Skill. Dilys grew up in Sedbergh and was for a time head of Garsdale School. Elizabeth is a Garsdale native and together they make an excellent partnership. Anthea continues to conduct most interviews in Dentdale.

Transcribing makes particular demands and we have been lucky to find helpers with the time, patience and skill to do this painstaking work. We are especially grateful to Shirley Tebay who transcribed many of the earlier recordings, and to Gill Newport who currently undertakes the task.

In the early days we used a simple tape recorder but, thanks to the generosity of the Neighbourhood Forum, we now have two excellent digital recording machines. Neville Allen manages the technical side of things and willingly gives his time to see that recordings are safely copied and inventoried.

Managing the archive has been a growing task and we owe thanks to Bryan Hinton for his meticulous work in the early days. Elspeth Griffiths took over the role and has helped in any number of other ways, sharing her wide knowledge of Sedbergh and its people.

Thanks are due to Kate Cairns for her contribution as the Society's secretary; to Diane Elphick for contributing her research skills and knowledge of local history; also to Maureen Lamb for her continued help and encouragement.

Most important of all, we give sincere thanks to all our interviewees. After all, you are the ones who have been 'telling it like it was'.

Photo credits

The photographs between pages 76 and 77 are reproduced by kind permission. The letter codes A to F at the end of each photo caption indicate the families and collections from which the pictures have been sourced.

A: Boulton family
B: Sedbergh and District History Society collection
C: Eliza Forder collection
D: Shirley Tebay collection
E: Ellison family
F: Mary Cowperthwaite family

Introducing our contributors

There are no fewer than sixty nine contributors to this book, each of them interviewed in the twenty one years between 1994 and 2015. Sadly, but not surprisingly since a number were born in the early years of the twentieth century, many have not lived to see their unique recollections in print. We are sure that their families and friends will treasure these voices from the past.

But happily many are alive and kicking! We would like to introduce you to a representative number of the sixty nine who have put on record their memories of dales life a generation or two back. We cannot detail them all here, though a full list appears below. But we can give readers an idea of the variety of background and range of experience on which we have been able to draw.

Since farming is the main industry in the dales it is to be expected that farmers' voices are prominent. The oldest, John Pratt, was born in Grisedale in 1905 and remembers the excitement of seeing the first motor cars to venture into the dales. Miles ('Miley') Taylor, born in 1923 at Butterpots, Deepdale, and Tom Sedgwick, born in 1917 at Spice Gill, Cowgill, are among the many who tell of hard life on small traditional farms, while Helga Frankland and Ingram Cleasby, both born in 1920, speak from a broader experience and wider horizons. A later generation, of which Leslie Robinson (1930), Dick Harrison (1934) and Kenneth Cragg (1936) are representative, lived through and recall the revolution in farming which saw the scythe replaced by the rotory mower and the horse by the tractor.

Many who started in farming diversified into other occupations. For example, Albert Fothergill (1923) ran a piggery before building a substantial business making concrete blocks in Dent. Garth Steadman (1945) became an award-winning retail butcher in Sedbergh. Fred Taylor ran a cheese-making business at Farfield. Helga Frankland and Ingram Cleasby, already mentioned, rose to the top of their chosen professions, Helga as a distinguished scientist and Ingram as Dean of Chester Cathedral.

Alongside the farmers and those with dual occupations were the skilled tradesmen and professionals. Neville Balderston (1924), joiner; Jack Dawson (1922), coal merchant; Eddie Smith (1949), publican and shop keeper; Brian Goad (1942), funeral director; Dennis Whicker (1951), policeman; George Handley (1937), teacher; and many more. Every one of them offers a unique glimpse of life in a diverse community on the cusp of social change.

And then there are the women! Perhaps, in the end, they emerge as the real stars of this book. Isabel ('Cissy') Middleton (1914), farmer with her husband Jim, egg merchant, champion butter maker, church organist and pig-foot pie specialist; Betty Harper (1920), head of Garsdale school; Mary Ellison (1909), farmer's wife, hay rake maker and Cowgill shop keeper; Betty Hartley, farmer, handknitter and renowned cake baker; Freda Trott (1919), piano teacher, munitions worker at Farfield, author and local historian… and, again, many more. They say a woman's work is never done, but rarely have the stories of their work been told with such natural flair and good humour.

But all work and no play would make an inadequate book. Men and women together tell tales of dancing and dating, church and chapel life, magic lantern and cinema, charabanc outings, and all the fun of Dent Fair. Sixty nine voices from our dales communities, telling what life was like for them and their generation.

A full list of the 69 who have been 'telling it like it was':

Dennis Abbott, John Airey, Mary Airey, Mary Allen, Judith Allison

Neville Balderston, David Boulton, Stanley Bracken

Reg Charnley, Ingram Cleasby, Tom Cornthwaite, Mary Cowperthwaite, Kenneth Cragg

Jack Dawson, Jean Donald, Bob Ellison, George Ellison, Mary Ellison

Albert Fothergill, Helga Frankland

Isobel German, Mary Gladstone, Brian Goad, Richard Goodyear

George Handley, Betty Harper, Dick Harrison, Betty Hartley, Hazel Haygarth, Kitty Howard, David Hutchinson

Cecil Iveson, Peter Iveson

Myles Jackson

Dick Kevan, Jenny Kiddle

Kevin Lancaster, Ben Lyon

Bessie Mason, Alan Mattinson, Cissy Middleton, Elizabeth 'Tizza' Middleton, Eva Middleton, Jack Middleton, Jim Middleton, Marjorie Middleton, Billy Milburn

Chris Payne, Dennis Pratt, John Pratt

Isobel Raw, Austin Robinson, Leslie Robinson, Jean Rochford, Tom Rycroft

Tom Sedgwick, Duncan Shuttleworth, Eddie Smith, Isobel Stacey, Garth Steadman

Fred Taylor, Miley Taylor, Robert Taylor, Shirley Tebay, Freda Trott, Bob Turner

Doris Waller, Dennis Whicker, Willie Whitwell

CHAPTER 1

Childhood

Freedom – Learner drivers –
Hunting and fishing – Working for pocket money –
Learning skills at home... and on the farm –
Help in the home – Family life and death –
Entertainments and treats –
Christmas

When we look back on our lives, childhood seems to hold a special place in our memories. Speaking about their early years our interviewees have given richly detailed accounts of work and play, family life and how it felt to be young in our dales in the early and middle decades of the twentieth century. Some of these experiences are universal. Children still fish in becks, help at home and on farms, and roam the countryside. Other descriptions, though, show how much life has changed for young people since those times. In the days of horses and Tilley lamps, when large families were common and work was mostly done by hand, childhood was often tough. It could also be amazingly, gloriously free.*

Freedom!

I'd a lovely childhood! Because there were lots of children around, not like now when there are very few! And we seemed to be free to go anywhere we liked, we could roam anybody's land, we used to be on the fells or river or making something, building fires or tents or making swings. **Betty Harper** b.1920

We were always keen on rabbiting and bird nesting, we'd set off Sunday morning and we wouldn't come back till six or seven o'clock at night when we got hungry. Nobody worried about it, nobody was going to run away with you. **Alan Mattinson** b.1934

We used to have the run of everything, go out at nights, and play in the holidays and climb up the gills, and we used to go into Gawthrop cave and High Hall cave, and go into the gill and climb up. It was really quite peaceful. Nowadays we'd think it quite dangerous for children to do that on their own, but that's the sort of thing we did. And bicycles, of course. **Marjorie Middleton** b.1913

Especially in summertime a lot of them used to come down, and if they had bicycles, ride on their bicycles round about, and we used to chat, we used to have lots of fun really because there was a lot of young ones together, it was a real gathering place at Garsdale Hall. **Mary Cowperthwaite** b.1924

We would cycle all over the place and our parents weren't worried because there wasn't all that much traffic around. **Mary Gladstone** b.1926

Ling [heather] was great fun because when we got a full load I remember Elsie and I, we must have got awfully dusty, one Saturday afternoon we spent the whole of the time bouncing on this ling, which was lovely! If you've never bounced on ling, you've never lived! **Freda Trott** b.1919

It was a wonderful childhood. When we were fairly young my younger brother and I used to go up the river Rawthey wearing gym shoes and bathing costumes, swimming through the pools and splashing through the rocks and clambering up the small waterfalls, quite unattended, but I suppose we would be perhaps eleven by then, and my younger brother and I had the same kinds of tastes, rearing frogs and all that kind of thing, and so we tended to play together. My father was, well men in general didn't have much to do with babies in those days, but he was very good with children of the age to play hide and seek, go in the woods, and he made bows and arrows for us. **Helga Frankland** b.1920

> *Before I started school I wasn't really aware that there were lots of other children all over the world*

It was a fairly isolated life that I had as a child. I remember quite well before I started school not really being aware that there were other children, I didn't really envisage the fact that there were lots and lots of us over the world. Mother couldn't drive so, unlike modern kids, I wasn't carted around from one social event to another. **Kevin Lancaster** b.1959

George Handley's grandfather had started the coal merchant business which later became known as Dawson's coal yard in Sedbergh.

I used to go down to the coal yard quite a bit and ride around in the coal wagons going up to the farms in the dales, particularly in winter. It was great fun because the farm lanes were pretty treacherous in those days… And I used to walk quite a bit on my own and go on the fell on my own. I became very interested in languages and used to take a little notebook with me and note down all the things for which I didn't know the French word, all the flowers and all the things that were growing in the lane, and note down those words. **George Handley** b.1937

I learnt to swim in the river and there was about four pools around the area and a lot of youngsters, most of us, had swum in the river. And there was one in the Clews at Rawthey down below Settlebeck, the meeting of the waters in the Lune and Rawthey, and then there was quite a nice pool above Killington bridge which we swam in, and then there was Bond's Holme wood above Broadrain Mill. We swam there and we used to build a fire and go down and roast potatoes and whatnot and end up having a feast. We were into our teens, the boys and girls as they were, there was nothing untoward and it's amazing really because there was no… I mean they used to get dressed with towels round and sometimes towels used to drop and you saw what you shouldn't but nobody ever bothered…

We used to go into Park Wood, which is just over Middleton bridge, and we used to pitch this tent up and we used to build a fire and we had our picnic. And in them days I collected birds' eggs, it was legal in them days, and I had over eighty different varieties, and we used to climb trees and look for birds' nests and I remember climbing one tree, thinking it was a magpie's, and put my hand in and three young squirrels shot out! Red squirrels! We used to go in a morning, we'd be there, mother never worried because there were never any problems in them days, and we used to enjoy ourselves and rough it all. **Leslie Robinson** b.1930

"We played in the gasworks yard and I used to go home covered in tar"

I lived close to Kings Yard [Sedbergh] so I could drop in. I'd drop in to Sedgwick's wood yard sometimes, and just watch the men working, using their circular saw to cut up wood. Sometimes I was allowed to turn the grindstone. I'd drop in and watch Mr George Law mixing his dough for making bread and putting it into the ovens. I'd drop into Ratcliffe's smithy to watch him shoeing horses, and we were welcomed and nobody threw us out. It was quite a pleasant way of spending the day in the school holidays. Wednesday was market day, you see, and the farmers used to come into town, and they'd bring their horses to be shoed on Wednesdays. I remember farmers bringing their horses to Ratcliffe's smithy in Kings Yard, and the smell, the smells of the smithy, the smell of burning hoof when he puts the shoes on, and the smells of the furnace…

One of my best friends at the National School was John Flint, the son of the local gasworks manager. Now the gasworks was at the bottom of New Street, just below the Methodist Chapel, and John and I used to play quite a lot in this gasworks yard. There was a big gas holder at the back, and a big stack of coke in front of the gas holder, and somewhere at the side there was a pile of spent oxide that was being re-aerated. We just used to play in the gasworks yard and I used to go home covered with tar. Grandmother used to be very annoyed, but still it was fun. **Peter Iveson** b.1938

Yes, yes, it was a happy time! Well there was nothing else! You'd got to be happy, happy with your little lot. **Albert Fothergill** b.1923

Learner drivers

In the early days cars were still quite a novelty. If you were lucky enough to have a go at driving, that was really exciting, and never mind rules and regulations!

Charlie Metcalfe had a coal business and he used to pick the children up in Grisedale and I used to help Charlie with the coal. I used to hold the bags while he filled them up, and then we'd to go off and deliver and he'd say 'Right, you can drive my Austin back', and that's how I learnt to drive. He didn't pay me but he'd let me drive!… I went to work for George Dinsdale at Swarthgill [Garsdale] leading manure every Saturday, and what the big highlight was, he had what they called a land-cart, a car with the rear end cut off and a body put onto it, and we used to put two heaps of muck on so we got a lot of drives. And he used to say 'don't put much on', but that was the reason, so we could tear down the fields, because when I was nine year old I could drive and change gear and everything. **Dennis Pratt** b.1935

> *I had a gun when I was eleven years old*

[My son] Edward was always a keen tractor chap, you know. One day we'd left it at the top of a field, and somebody had left the brake off. Edward saw it going, he ran and jumped on and got it stopped… He would drive the tractor with the hay. You see, he wasn't so big and he couldn't see over the top of the hay, so we put rakes up at either side of the gate so's he could see where the gate was. He was only about eight! **Betty Hartley** b.1913

They shared the childminding between them, mother and father. I was sat on the seat of the vehicle, horse rake or whatever, when father was going round and he said I had to be tied on because I tended to fall asleep. **Kevin Lancaster** b.1959

Hunting and fishing

I think I had a gun when I was eleven years old and I used to go rabbiting. And I've always had a dog, I always liked terriers. **Austin Robinson** b.1942

Where J M Pratts are still, once upon a time they used t' come round [to Garsdale] with a Morris commercial vehicle with sides that used to open up, and they used to sell everything! And buy! They'd buy rabbits from yer! I was quite a dab hand with the catapult! One of the lads that lived behind the garage at Swarthgill, he was a dab hand at making catapults with car inner tube tyres, the red stuff, and he showed me how to pick catapult sticks out the hedge and say, 'No, that won't be ready for about five months', and he'd fasten it round the top two prongs with string to teach it t' grow fer the right shape. I don't know whether you would call it skill, I think it was just adaptability. [Pratts] would give us, oh, about nine pence, something like that, they used t' buy them off you. I know if you bought one it's likely the same rabbit that came back, but by then they were one and thre'pence! **Bob Turner** b.1933

Moles and rabbits… well there was black-and-white 'uns, there was bald 'uns, there was all sorts. And I remember when I was in me teens, most I catched was about a thousand. Aye, that was what used to be me pocket money. And t' moles… well me father set me off catching moles and he med some traps and that, and me Uncle Jack from Deepdale Head (he used to go down south when he was in his young days, catching moles) and he was come to show me how to catch 'em. And

I got about three hundred... Oh, I didn't get owt for catching moles. Tek t' money for t' rabbits. And they were a good price once over, up to five shilling a couple. But t' early part o' t' time I used to tek 'em up to George Ellis at East Cowgill. He used to go at Thursday, down to Morecambe wi t' hoss and cart, and tek these rabbits, but he never gev me above one and thre'pence apiece, howiver good they were; and they were fat – kidneys were covered wi' fat – and he said t' rabbit fat was no good! But anyway as time went on there was another feller come round from Barrowford – Wicks they called him. And he gev a better price and so he got 'em you see... And then maybe I started keeping a few hens for meself. If I'd ten shilling a week profit I thought I was a millionaire! **Jim Middleton** b.1913

' *People in the town don't know the difference between a chicken and a rabbit!* '

We kept ferrets. Aye, we allus had two or three ferrets. Aye, well that used to be our pocket money when we were lads, was the rabbits. They were only about sixpence each, but sixpence went quite a long way in those days. We had a port for them. A chap used to come up from Burnley and collect rabbits and fowls, and take them back. Yes, he used the skins, aye. I asked him, I said, 'What do you do with all these when you get them to Burnley?'. 'Well', he said, 'there's a place there called Turf Moor. They play football… We have a stall there and we sell chicken sandwiches! Most people in the town don't know the difference between a chicken and a rabbit!'. And they don't! But that was back before the war, back in the twenties and thirties. I don't suppose there'd be a lot of inspectors around in those days. **Willie Whitwell** b.1914

As a boy I had a round of rabbits in Dent, I used to sell ten a week at half a crown apiece, dressed rabbits, to people in Dent village. Regular orders were these, and I had a regular order for ten a week an' I used to try and sell a few more sometimes. **Kenneth Cragg** b.1936

We were always keen on rabbiting. Just when I left school at the end of the war, the butcher in Sedbergh, for a really good rabbit he'd pay five shillings. With the rabbiting money I bought my first bicycle from Len Haygarth's garage at Dent, a three-speed Hercules, it cost £14 brand new. **Alan Mattinson** b.1934

We used to fish a lot at times, in t' river Lune like, and we used to fish places where we hadn't to fish. We got chased once by t' old boy at Burrow Hall. What was it they called him? Fenwick. And old Fenwick used to wear a smoking cap. Chased us. We were grappling trout in Leck Beck and he shouted at us – we had school hats on you see, them little green hats, and Dr Paget-Tomlinson was chairman of the magistrates and he gave everybody a stern lecture. **Cecil Iveson** b.1907

> *One of my jobs was to brush Lady Bentinct's dogs' teeth with Milton*

Well, salmon, of course, long ago [around 1920] salmon used t' come up dale an' a lot of these young lads used t' go poachin', an' they would land in a big salmon. I 'ad one brother that used t' tek all roe an' used t' cure it, an' fishermen would like t' buy this roe that 'e'd cured, for fishin' with, but yer know it was a thing yer got a bit tired of if you'd too much but oh, they would come in wi' a huge salmon at times 'cause there was such a lot came up. **Cissy Middleton** b.1914

We used to go grappling trout, that was one of our hobbies as boys. I can always remember going grappling trout in the Scandal, which is a river in Ravenstonedale, and on a good Sunday we could catch sixty, you know, and then we used to get sixpence for them off Stan Smith, he would put 'em on the menu at the Black Swan. **Garth Steadman** b.1945

Working for pocket money

I had a little job. I used to go to Kendal with Rowley Sanderson on a Saturday and that was the best job I ever had, it was a shilling for the day, collecting parcels for deliveries to the shops in Dent. Rowley Sanderson was a carrier. I was twelve. He had a small wagon, a Bedford... I worked on farms, I would probably creosote a hen hut fer somebody fer tuppence, a penny or tuppence. **Albert Fothergill** b.1923

I used to go to Underley Hall [Kirby Lonsdale]. Lady Bentinck had dogs and one of my jobs was to brush their teeth every day with Milton. **Neville Balderston** b.1924

Learning skills at home...

My grandmother was a knitter who knitted with the four needles – she knitted socks and things – and she taught me to knit when I was three years old, and I've been knitting one sort or other on and off ever since. **Betty Hartley** b.1913

The night nursery was down a very small step to the day nursery and we used this to make an incline for our Hornby engines to go up, and my father took advantage of this saying 'Now let's find out what the rate of climb is', and he did the maths with us and of course we were interested. **Helga Frankland** b.1920

...and on the farm

Yes, we all had our jobs. You set off when you were about four year old maybe and you had to get the sticks and coals in ready for next morning. We weren't allowed to use the axe but the sticks would be chopped and we would have to go and bring them in. We rather worked by the daylight than the dark because them days we didn't have electric, we only had oil lamps and candles so in winter we would get up later but we didn't have any jobs in a morning, the sticks and coals were brought in in the afternoon when we got home from school. As I got older, about seven, we had hens and pigs but not many, just sometimes one pig for killing in the hull [the pigsty] and a few hens, and we'd have to go and feed the hens before we went to school, and maybe the pig, and the same when we came home from school. Then when you got older still you would have to milk two cows before you went to school or in winter you would have to go to the out barn and feed the young stock, that would be before you went to school and then again when you came home again at night. The jobs varied, I think that was the interest of farming. You never objected to it 'cos you didn't think you could, not as today you would say 'No, I'm not doing that', but not in

> *Farmers' sons, they weren't kept as ornaments*

those days, and you didn't feel bad about it because that was just life. Nothing was a chore, we'd always plenty to do but I never remember complaining that I mustn't do this or oh I don't want to do that, and we never used the word that we hear today – bored – 'cos we never were, even though we didn't have television and all that. **Kenneth Cragg** b.1936

It was hard, yes it was hard. Farmers' sons, they weren't kept as ornaments, you had to do your bit. I can remember when my father was mowing I used to get up when I was ten or eleven and have to go to rake off for him before I went to school. And then a few years after I once told a teacher, 'You fellers didn't realise but we'd done a day's work, cows to milk and hens to feed, before we went to school', and he said he didn't know, he didn't realise that. These teachers were all out of town. **Austin Robinson** b.1942

I used to trail up to Butterpots [Deepdale] when we left school, not to play because playing wasn't fashionable in those days, we had work to do and I'd probably help [Miley Taylor] with his jobs, but no, there was no play really, we weren't brought up to play, we were brought up to work… you'd be feeding hens or calves or something. **Albert Fothergill** b.1923

Ever since we were little we'd all our jobs t' do. Right from being small, even if we were little, we'd t' go and fetch a few sticks in. Even when we started school we'd all our little jobs t' do – go an' feed a few 'ens, feed a lamb or two, feed a calf – whatever there was goin' we was allus brought up t' do little jobs. When we got t' about six or seven years old and when it came t' summertime an' we'd to start thinkin' 'bout 'aytime, we all bought a rake, a small rake, an' they were made by Willie Middleton o' joiners at Dent, which were famous for rake makin'. Of course men 'ad their big rakes but we little ones, we only wanted one height of ourselves, which wasn't so big an' not so many teeth in it. **Cissy Middleton** b.1914

On the farm we had a next door neighbour who always grew little bits of oats and roll crop and he used to plough with horses. Now I learnt to plough with a horse at eight years old with a swing plough. He had two very quiet horses which were good for me and I was quite a strongish lad at eight years old so I was able to plough with a horse, with two horses and a swing plough. **Leslie Robinson** b.1930

When you went home at night you 'ad your tea and you got changed and you went out and you did a bit of work. There was no 'omework, I've never done any 'omework in me life. Up to about twelve, thirteen, you 'ad to start doing a bit of work. Farm boys, it was all the same. And then when tractors came along you couldn't wait to get 'ome! I was eleven. Me father, 'e wasn't mechanically minded at all, 'e'd been brought up with 'orses, and 'e didn't like it, but I took to it like a duck to water. I remember mowing and things like that, yeah. You'd have got locked up nowadays wi' health and safety, but it's the way it was. **Austin Robinson** b.1942

Help in the home

We weren't driven t' work, we were just expected to do our duty and we knew it was our duty. **Bessie Mason** b.1911

Ooh yes, we'd all our own jobs to do. Well I know what my job was! We'd an old earth toilet wi' two holes at t' top an' that was one of my jobs. An' cleaning the knives and forks was the other one. Because they were yellow, they weren't like they are today. No, no, you 'ad to clean 'em with Brasso and then wash 'em in t' sink after you'd cleaned them. And the others, the others had their own jobs as well and they 'ad to do 'em, there was no no-ing, 'I'm not doing 'em'. **Isobel Raw** b. 1924

We'd 'ave t' clean our clogs, 'cause it was allus clogs, yer know, there was no slippers an' fancy shoes in those days! There was no wellingtons, it was all clogs wi' carkers on [metal strips on the soles]. An' of course when it was winter time they would jus', what we call, ball up wi' snow – you know, they would jus' stick together an' you would get big lumps on yer clogs an' you would jus' 'ave t' go up t' wall an' give it a good kick an' knock it off, otherwise you would wobble over! **Cissy Middleton** b.1914

Family life – and death

You see there was such a lot… There was ten at Wardses. You know that little cottage, last one [in Cowgill] before you go up to t' viaducts? There was ten childer. She had ten kiddies, Mrs Ward, and her husband worked on t' railway. Of course t' bigger ones were getting left school when t' little ones were little. But how they all lived in that house I just don't know. There was six up at Dale Head and old Harry Campbell's at Carley had six. You know, everybody seemed to have about half a dozen. **Mary Ellison** b.1909

At one time there was about thirteen children going out o' Grisedale to Lunds School. There was three quite large families in Grisedale. And there was eight farms in Grisedale at that time. **John Pratt** b.1905

I had three sisters and three brothers but then I had another brother who died at the age of eighteen months. I remember seeing him in a small coffin in my parents' bedroom. My sister Mary Margaret, she actually brought me up and looked after me a great deal. Well, me being the last of the seven and her being some nine years older, she got the job of looking after me. **David Hutchinson** b.1920

There were thirteen of us and I was the eighth. An' me mum died when I was twelve. Me elder sisters were (looking after the younger ones). Me elder sister was ten years older than meself so it went the same, when I was eight or ten she'd be eighteen and that sort of thing. **Cissy Middleton** b.1914

In the days before modern medicine and the National Health Service life was more precarious. Illnesses were harder to treat, and war and epidemics played their part in pushing up the death rate. 1919 was an especially bad time, with the so-called 'Spanish flu' epidemic following on the hardships of the First World War.

[My father] got TB. He was in the British army and was invalided out. He died before I was born. The flu epidemic, that killed my father. But my mother died of flu as well, when I was eight. She died in 1927. **Freda Trott** b.1919

When t' Spanish flu was on, you know there was a lot of men died, wasn't there? I knew one or two families left with seven children an' left to bring 'em up, you know. Well they got brought up. **Bessie Mason** b.1911

The nearest doctor was in Sedbergh, Dr Scott Jackson, and I remember he had to come out once on Christmas Day. Mum and I had bread and jam for our Christmas dinner, and Dr Scott Jackson came out to see dad because he was so poorly. He used to say 'I'm afraid I'll have to have a shilling for the Government', a prescription then was a shilling. He was quite embarrassed because he knew we were struggling. **Mary Airey** b.1945

> *I never missed a film... Cowboys, Robin Hoods, everybody was Tarzans*

Well I was just into my teens really. I used to keep house for a while before me mum died because of her ill health. I used to do the housework, washing, cooking. I was quite a dab hand at a Sunday lunch. I was at school, yes, but later on I did get a part-time job while I was still at school, I worked at one of the schools in Sedbergh, Winder House; it was just, like, cleaning up of a night time to get a bit of pocket money. I have now one brother, an older brother, one younger sister. I did have an elder sister but she died just before I was born. **Judith Allison** b.1954

Entertainments and treats

I can remember the school [Howgill] being what seemed packed with people, and mother working the Magic Lantern and watching Peter Pan with great glee! It seemed so romantic, Peter Pan, it was lovely! **Freda Trott** b. 1919

Sedbergh Picture House was in the building now occupied by Westwood Books and proved a big attraction.

I never used t' miss a film! It was only thre'pence! Cowboys, all the Robin Hoods were done, all the Tarzans, everybody was Tarzans, 'The Man in the Iron Mask' and anything that was done, fencing, so you went home all the way with yer gabardine mac fastened at the neck as a cloak and cut a stick out of the hedge and fence all the way home! Bruised knuckles. **Bob Turner** b.1933

We used to have a day at Morecambe after haytime and that was the highlight of the year. **Alan Mattinson** b.1934

> *A trip to Morecambe was like going to the moon!*

We used to have every year a Sunday school trip from the Methodist Sunday school and we always went to Morecambe and we used to have two of Braithwaites' charas [charabancs] as we called them and go by the old road, no motorway in those days of course to Morecambe, it seemed a long way, and have a full day in Morecambe with a sort of lunch in one of the Methodist Church schoolrooms. Other outings, yes, my father had a car and occasionally we used to go into the Lakes or we'd go for a picnic onto Fair Mile or onto Killington Fell, places like that. **George Handley** b.1937

Sunday School outings were very important in the community. In the early days, in the twenties, oh a trip to Morecambe was a wonderful thing. Probably like going to the moon now! Yes it was a very jolly day! [Holidays were] limited to a week. With my father and mother, and the three of us, William, Jean and myself. Yes we would go to Morecambe, to a boarding house, on the front if possible. And we took all our eatables for the week and the landlady cooked them for us. Bacon and eggs and so on and so forth. Very happy days! **Jack Dawson** b.1922

Our treat when we were little was me dad used to always take us on the train, we used to go by bus, catch the train from Oxenholme, and we'd go down to Blackpool. We just went on anything we could – lots of ice creams, candy floss an' we always used to come back with a nodding dog – one of those dogs that used to nod up and down. **Judith Allison** b.1954

I always remember the first holiday I had, I think I was about twelve and I had just completed a month's haymaking, and I went to Cleveleys, Blackpool, for a week's holiday and I took my haytime wage with me. It was two pounds and I came back and I was skint, I'd spent all my two pounds. I was broken-hearted, I never wanted another holiday because I couldn't afford it, spent all my money on silly games and things I'd never seen before. I'd wasted it all. **Albert Fothergill** b.1923

Christmas

Sanker Davis used to produce the nativity play, and as I grew up a bit I was the angel Gabriel. We used to do it at midnight [on Christmas Eve] down at the Vale of Lune, that very narrow church… Joe Sanker Davis loved gadgets and I was dressed in a sheet as the angel Gabriel to lead this procession, and he had made me a beautiful star strapped to my head with wires down my back… I had wings, and my hands were under this sheet holding the two wires onto a battery. It was dark of course, we just had candles, walking down that aisle, and the first king, a big boy, stood on my sheet and suddenly this star went out and I was jerked backwards! I have accused two of the boys and they keep saying 'No, it wasn't me!'…

We went to Dent church to give the nativity play, must have been an evening, and in those days they had an organ that had to be pumped, so there was a choir boy who stood there and he pumped. And quite a long service as well. When we came to sing the last hymn, 'While Shepherds Watched' or whatever it was, we started singing quite merrily and suddenly the organ went err, err, err and it got weaker and weaker because he had gone to sleep! And so I set off to laugh…and the three wise men…

"You had to tek a bit of coal in, and you would get a mincepie and some ginger beer"

well once you start laughing you can't stop, can you, especially school children! Oh! But that was the highlight of the evening! This poor little soul, he'd been there pumping, and perhaps it was the sermon! **Jean Rochford** b. *c*1927

Christmas was a big occasion. Well it is for any kid, isn't it? With 'indsight now we didn't get much, but you didn't know much, did you? We used to get an apple and an orange and mebbe some plasticine and a book, and I know one year I got the very smallest size Meccano set, well that was fantastic, fantastic! New Year's morning I used to go round letting t' New Year in, and get sixpences. Just go in and wish 'em a happy and prosperous New Year. Mrs Haygarth at Banks Farm used to give me two and sixpence which was a lot of money then. I was expected to go, you know, there were reminders before. Some of 'em you had to tek a bit of coal in, and you would get a mincepie and some ginger beer, 'appen a bit of Christmas cake. **Dick Harrison** b.1934

There was none of this 'I want this' or 'I want that'. You used one of the boys' stockings because they were big stockings for footballing, so you'd get more in. And you'd get a few nuts, probably an apple and a tangerine, a few sweets and then you got something to wear. There was no toys and things. **David Hutchinson** b.1920

We used to go round all the school houses carol singing with Joe Sanker Davis. I suppose Joe thought the boys would come up and put money in the bag if there were girls there, they were chiefly girls, you see, because the older boys had gone off to the army. Then one year we were invited to Gate [Dent]. That was lovely! Afterwards we got tea and mincepies and we could eat more than one! **Jean Rochford** b. *c*1927

The best place to carol sing was behind the Red Lion [Sedbergh]. Because they used to 'ave to come out of the back and walk across to the toilets. And in them days it was all men that smoked, and entry was all in darkness, and we'd sing and they'd come out of the bar and all the smoke used to come out, you couldn't see owt, and they used to say 'What you doing, lad?'. We'd say, 'carol singing'. And they'd give me a penny or so… But it was that pitch black, once or twice we used to get a florin instead of a penny. We used to think, somebody's going to wonder where their money's gone! **John Airey** b.1942

CHAPTER 2

Schooldays

Getting there – Time out –
'Makin' us use our brains' – Discipline –
'Tig…skipping…marbles…hopscotch' –
No school dinners!

Recollections in this chapter mainly cover the decades from 1910 to the 1950s. Dentdale had two schools, one in Dent and one in Cowgill. Garsdale also had two, one in the village and one at Lunds. Howgill and other outlying areas were similarly served. These schools took all ages from infants to seniors. Sedbergh had private and state schools. Private institutions included two small dame schools; a preparatory school, which moved to Settlebeck House in 1922; and Sedbergh School, a boys' boarding school dating back to the 16th century.

National and British schools dated back to the 19th century when the Church of England supported the National School movement and the Nonconformists followed with their British Schools, both subsequently absorbed into the state system. Sedbergh had both, eventually amalgamated to become Sedbergh County Primary School based at Settlebeck. Settlebeck was expanded further to become Sedbergh Secondary Modern, and with the introduction of comprehensive education it changed again to become Settlebeck High School. For children who passed the 11-plus exam there was Queen Elizabeth School in Kirkby Lonsdale, which offered boarding facilities for children like those from Dent who otherwise faced a difficult journey.

Getting there

No taxis in those days! We had to exercise our legs. **Betty Hartley** b.1913

It's supposed to be from Deepdale Head three miles to Dent. We would walk, and then we had bicycles and we'd perhaps ride back on the carrier. See, everybody else was walking so you'd plenty of company. We didn't think anything about it. **Elizabeth Middleton** b.1915

I went to Cowgill… and we used t' know if we would be late by looking up on t' railway. If nine o'clock train came then we knew we were late!… I 'ad to walk two and a half miles, some of 'em had to walk as far as four and a half. **Bessie Mason** b.1911

This generally involved walking down the roads and over the fells, but for some it was rather more adventurous.

I went to Lowgill School about a year and had to cross the river Lune… There was a box on wires. Aye, there was a rope pulley. One of the lasses from the school used to set us down to the box and me dad used to be there to meet us, to see us across. But one day he was not there and she'd turned back before we got to the box, and so I decided I would go across on the wires, two hands on the top wires and both feet on the bottom wires, and slided across till I got to the end. If I'd dropped in that would have been it! Me parents was a bit upset that I'd done that and they decided to send us down to Howgill School. And me brother then was only four year old, and there was other scholar lads nearby, neighbours, and we all went down to Howgill School, walked it… be about two and a half mile. **Stanley Bracken** b.1911

From the 1920s on some children began to benefit from more modern means of transport.

After I left Cowgill school in 1924 they started bringing 'em from Ribblehead [by train]. Kiddies walked down from t' station [Dent] to t' school and walked back again at night… they were walking down right from Dent Head, on the top. That was a long way to school! **Mary Ellison** b.1909

It was your first courting, even at eleven!

It was a huge Austin 16 that seated about eight. It had these little fold-up seats in the middle between the front of the car and the back! He [Tom Dinsdale, known as Tom Cock to the children] used to have to come down twice. Once you lived more than a mile from the school you were entitled to the school car. As he went past Longholme he'd toot his horn to let you know that he'd gone past. He'd go past about twenty past eight with the first ones, and then he'd be back about twenty five to nine and you'd just get in there before class!… You weren't allowed to eat. He had very sensitive ears to sweet papers! Each time you looked forward there was a pair of eyes looking at you in his reversing mirror to see what was going on. And he had this strange porkpie hat that he wore, and as round a face as you could have imagined… But if anyone was ill and he thought he could get them all in the car, you'd get those days where it was like the back seat of the pictures! It was your first courting! Even at eleven! Scrambling about in the back of the car with 'What are you all up to?' **Bob Turner** b.1933

I passed into Queen Elizabeth's, Kirkby Lonsdale, in September 1918 and was there from 1918 to 1922. I cycled down on a Monday and went into digs and cycled back on a Friday night, on a push bike. Train service was no good and there was no buses. **Cecil Iveson** b.1907

Sedbergh's very unusual in that it had both a British and a National School but they had been united in the fifties. When I started, the infants were in the British School and the primary children were in the National School building. Settlebeck had been bought for the post-elevens. At the British School the food was vile, unbearably awful, you wouldn't have given it to a pig… I thought until I was sixteen school represented society as a whole, or the 45 per cent that had passed the eleven plus, but it was very striking that from sixteen and over I was the only farmer left. All the ones that were my social equals, as I call them, were out getting jobs and I was there with the college lecturers' children, the teachers' children, who were probably not naturally my colleagues in the same way as the ones I knew when I was sixteen… I think a lot of people had ambitions for me but I don't think anybody really bothered to ask me what my own views were. I was put in for Cambridge and I'm sure I would have got into Trinity College if I'd had a third year in the sixth, but I wasn't properly prepared. Southampton was my second choice but I'd never spent a night away from Fellgate and Southampton University was more alien to me then than any foreign country would be to me now. After two weeks I came home, and thank God I did rebel, but mother never forgave me, never ever forgave me. **Kevin Lancaster** b.1959

> *I think we had a clock, but nobody ever looked at it*

I felt tied [when I started at Dent school]. I'd never been used to living where hours mattered, an' I had to be there at a certain time in a morning, which I didn't like, an' I had to leave at a certain time at night, and our whole life on the farm didn't rotate around a clock 'cos – well, I think we had one but nobody ever looked at it. So suddenly having my life governed was not particularly good. But on our way to school we used to tickle trout, 'cos we 'ad to walk a mile along the river side, and then on the way home we would do the same again. We didn't seem to have bailiffs and that them days, and we never took too many, you only got four or five for the breakfast on the odd occasion, so it was quite good. We had to walk right from the age of five and then when I got to about eleven I got a push-bike, and then when we went to Settlebeck we went by coach that used to pick us up every morning. **Kenneth Cragg** b.1936

> *They weren't very particular whether you went to school or you didn't*

Time out

Two things got in the way of regular schooling. In the winter it was bad weather, in the summer the priority was given to haytiming while the sun was shining.

We walked over from Grisedale for our schooling. We walked on the fell bottom and down some pastures and into Lunds, something like three mile. And we generally went wi' our clogs and kept our clogs on all day. We once were at school – there was four or five of us going at that time – and when we got home that day every one of us hadn't a dry rag on us. [There was a man] we called the whipper-in [attendance officer], Mr Matthew Sedgwick from Sedbergh, and he was sitting having his tea with my parents, and he says, 'Well, if your children doesn't come to school when it's wild I shall never say anything about it'. **John Pratt** b.1905

If it was a north wind it would block the road [Deepdale Head] with snow in ten minutes. It happened often in those days. I cut the road till I couldn't cut enough, cutting all the snow off the road, just in squares. [When we couldn't get to school] mother used to take us in reading. She was very anxious for us to be scholars and to fit us for our place in the world. **Elizabeth Middleton** b.1915

In the summer, in what we call the haytime season, we were allowed to come away from school in the afternoon, you know, to help get the hay in. **Billy Milburn** b.1938

When I got to be coming fourteen I don't think I went much that summer, because it was a bad summer and we'd a late haytime. And also it was about the end of the First World War. They weren't very particular whether you went to school or you didn't. **John Pratt** b.1905

There was one family had quite a lot of children and the mother's wash house was some way from the house, so the eldest boy was given time off school on a Monday to look after the small children whilst his mother did the washing. **Marjorie Middleton** b.1913

I left school when I was fourteen. I should have been fifteen but haytime started and me dad kept me off school. We had a visit from the truancy officer, a Mr Grimbleby from Wakefield, and he told me father that he was going to fine him so much a day, and he asked him what it was and [father] said 'Well, he's worth more than that at home!'. That would be the end of June and I should have left in August but I never went back. We never saw anybody [about it] again. **Austin Robinson** b.1942

> *Mr Teer made us work with our 'eads, which we'd never done before*

We were going to the National School, then at Easter they moved to Settlebeck, so documentation wasn't as thorough at t' Education Authority as they thought. Me dad 'ad 'ad some red letters threatening 'im if I didn't go to school, but when the school moved to Settlebeck he nivver 'ad no more, so I nivver went again. **Dick Harrison** b.1934

'Makin' us use our brains'

We started off in a morning with scripture, of course; and then arithmetic for our next lesson – I hated that. And then after that it followed on with either writing or reading or… everything. We'd to all knit a pair of stockings. We'd all to make something in sewing, and we had drawing and painting lessons. **Mary Ellison** b.1909

Mr Teer made us work wi' our 'eads, which we'd never done before. We 'adn't t' 'ave pencil an' paper, we'd t' work problems out in our 'eads, sums an' that, makin' us use our brains, I think. And music, he was very good on music. And he learned us 'ow to sing from t' tonic sol-fa, and he used to have us singing in parts, part-songs. He was very, very good – good at playing and good at teaching us. I mean, it's carried with me all me life, has that. Because when we joined t' church choir I could sing alto because we'd been learned 'ow to do it. **Cissy Middleton** b.1914

Nature lessons… Yes, we went outside. And we could usually tell the teacher some things they didn't know… And we used to dig her garden for her and so forth, we'd sooner do that than lessons. **Willie Whitwell** b.1914

I went to Dent till I was six and then I went to Cowgill till I was fourteen and left school then. You only went till you were fourteen unless you won a scholarship and I didn't want to go away anywhere so I didn't try!… They got up to eighty six in Cowgill School, with two teachers. And that's how I missed quite a few lessons, wi' looking after t' infants while they took t' middle ones. I often went into t' infant room and looked after them, just kept 'em amused, you know, and try to learn 'em bits o' things. **Mary Ellison** b.1909

Lunds School was rather primitive for what you learned. There was under-elevens and over-elevens. They were good days really. We had sums, arithmetic, writing was composition, nature, supposed to be science, but we lived with nature, the plant life, the birds' nests and so on. Every other Tuesday the boys over eleven went on the train from Garsdale Head to Hawes and did a day's joinery. I liked that. [The girls] did sewing, or perhaps knit. **Dennis Abbott** b.1926

I remember going on [from Howgill] to the British School and a whole sea of faces, and I was terrified. I was so terrified I once ran away! I hated school and I never really tried to do things as I should 'ave done! **Freda Trott** b.1919

I went to Miss Tetley's at Briar Lea, which was a house just up Long Lane. There

> *...this curious institution, the University of Sedbergh*

were two of these little Dame Schools in Sedbergh. Mrs Martin had one at the west end and Miss Tetley had this one at the east end. There were only about half a dozen of us there. She had a large table, in the room upstairs, and we all sat round it, different ages, I would think I would have been about seven, eight, and there were others, sometimes older and some younger. She used to give us dictation and we all sat round with our exercise books and she would have several books in front of her at different levels, you know, simple ones for the younger ones and more difficult words for the older ones, and she would read out a sentence from the relevant book and the relevant child would write that down, and then she would go on to the next one! How she didn't get muddled up, I don't know! **Mary Gladstone** b.1926

Helen and I went to a school for girls in Bowness and stayed there for going on for two years, and our parents realised that we weren't learning enough to get into, well, good girls' schools, sort of girls' public school type of thing, so they brought us home and we had lessons from a number of different people in Sedbergh. My father taught us history, her father taught us Latin, the retired chaplain of Sedbergh School taught us scripture and chemistry, which we were allowed to do in the school labs, which was quite a privilege! And various other masters taught us, and the retired headmistress, Dr Skeat of Baliol, she taught us English and French, and so it went on, and we chose to call this curious institution the University of Sedbergh! While we were doing it we had all sorts of privileges – swimming in the school baths, gym classes on Saturdays from Sergeant Stoker… It wasn't just a few of us, it was really a combination of Sedbergh children eleven, twelve years old, that sort of age and younger… but we got on pretty well because we did then get into what you might call 'good schools'. **Helga Frankland** b.1920

There was one teacher [at Dent], she was Miss Gladys Winder from the George and Dragon, I always loved her. It was like as if our dispositions seemed to fit each other. Oh yes, she was a marvellous teacher. And they put themselves out to help you and to negotiate with you, because I think children can be quite hostile. **Elizabeth Middleton** b.1915

Dent School was the best school in England! Miss Robinson was my teacher when I started at five years of age and thinking back she was an absolute lady, she was kind to us and good to us. I'd no complaints. **Albert Fothergill** b.1923

I loved it from the word go! I used a slate, and a chalk to write on it, and then you had a rubber, but of course spit helped too, to rub it out! We learnt to sing the alphabet, which I still can do! I taught my eldest grandchild, she knows the alphabet. The younger one, in spite of posh degrees, she doesn't know the alphabet. Same with counting and tables, we sang them! I still know my tables! **Jean Rochford** b. *c*1927

> *I didn't like all the teachers, but I liked school*

At playtime there was two yards. The girls went into the one at t' back of the school and we went into the one that came up to the road. And if in those days there was a car coming we used to all run out to the road to see the car. And we used to throw our hats on to the road for the cars to run over. And I can remember one boy just came to the road as the car was coming and he threw his hat on and it went on t' front of t' bonnet, and away it went with the car! He lost his hat! **John Pratt** b.1905

I rather liked school. I didn't like all the teachers, but I liked school. **Miley Taylor** b.1923

Many children never extended their education beyond local junior school, but some took the exams that enabled them to move on to secondary schools – Queen Elizabeth School at Kirkby Lonsdale, Sedbergh School, and (after 1949) Settlebeck.

In Standard Five you took the eleven-plus examination [introduced in 1944] and the successful ones went off to the Queen Elizabeth Grammar School in Kirkby Lonsdale. And those who didn't pass went up into Standard Six and then Standard Seven. They left school at fourteen. Mr Lilley took the top class; he was the headmaster. The boys in the top class seemed to spend a lot of time on woodwork. They were the only ones, I think, who used the woodwork room. And gardening, on a piece of land opposite the school. They didn't quite know what to do with them in those days after they'd failed the eleven-plus. **Peter Iveson** b.1938

I had to pass an exam to go to Sedbergh School and I had to take Latin lessons. My brothers Herbert, John and Lawrence, all four of us went. There was a scholarship which meant that the fees were all sort of worked in, and at that stage I didn't know how it was all financed, I just know that I went, and occasionally some money had to be paid out, but what I don't know. **David Hutchinson** b.1920

We wore clogs at Ravenstonedale but I remember when I went to grammar school we couldn't wear clogs, I was really pleased! **Mary Cowperthwaite** b.1924

I went to Ravenstonedale School for a short while. There was only five or six of us an' they closed it. So then for a year they bussed us to Newbiggin on Lune School until the numbers were back up at Ravenstonedale, an' then we went back… Mrs Dent was t' schoolteacher, there would probably be about twelve or thirteen of us then, but there was only two of us doing O-levels. **Garth Steadman** b.1945

It was their first assay into the larger world, when they moved down [to Settlebeck] from Dent. And there were people in Cowgill who hadn't been to Dent then! And people in Dent who hadn't been to Sedbergh. And they wore britches and clogs! **Dick Kevan** b.1914

When I went to take county minor exam, I thought 'I am not going to pass! I am not going to go to any other school! I want to leave school and that's all I want to do!'. **Freda Trott** b.1919

Well, lots of people were much better scholars than I was, y' see, so I really hadn't to compete with the world… There wasn't such thing as competing with the world because if you had a farm you just stayed on and worked. That was the policy. **Elizabeth Middleton** b.1915

The expectation was that you just went out to work to earn a living. Yes, in a way [school did equip you] but we just had to earn a living and that was it. We were self-keeping afterwards, we'd no social security. **Albert Fothergill** b.1923

I was fifteen when I left school. I always wanted to be a garage man, I have always been keen on mechanics, but in those days times were hard. I would have had to lodge in Kendal, my pay would have been thirty shillings a week and my parents couldn't afford to subsidise me, so it was no go. That's what I really wanted to be. **Alan Mattinson** b.1934

'I got caned most days, and I think I deserved it every time'

It was different then, in 1953, I mean there was always a job to go to. If you left one job there was another waiting. I mean there was always plenty of employment around the Sedbergh area. And you could get a job anywhere, you know, because there was a lot of building firms in the town. It's what I wanted to do, but I had no option but to work at home on the farm. I was never really a farming fanatic. I mean, I love contract work, I just love walling and hedging, but there was always work, plenty of work, because every farm in the district used to employ a man or two. Different to what it is now – a lot different. **Billy Milburn** b.1938

Discipline

There was one boy… we'd been doing something, and we all had to go up to this desk and hold our hands out to get the cane, but he wouldn't. We had an under-teacher called Miss Myers, but she was a hefty lass. And she just reached over the desk and got him by the hair and pulled him down till he was over the desk, and then made dust fly out of his pants! Next time she said 'Hold your hand out' he held it out! You'd done something and you got caned for it. You just got your just desserts. I got caned most days, I think, and looking back at it I deserved it every time. **Willie Whitwell** b.1914

Mr Teer taught t' lads manners. You know, he believed in a lot of manners which they hadn't in those days. T' boys had to touch their cap, you see, and 'Good morning, sir' and suchlike, where they would never think of it before if they were going through t' village. But he was very good. His look would be sufficient, but I remember once there was one lad yawnin' away an' 'e jus' got a duster an' 'e threw it at 'im! I think they knew 'e was well an' truly boss! **Cissy Middleton** b.1914

We had rather a severe schoolmaster and I think there was about nine or ten of us out of a class of about eleven, and every one of us got t' stick, for not doing our lessons. Well that night my hand was just partly black, he struck so hard at us. I went out and I was in tears. And I remember me granddad was going by with his hoss and cart with hay on. He'd been at Garsdale Station, Hawes Junction Station as it was in those days, for some hay, and if he'd had anybody to hold his hoss I think he would a' gone in and dealt with 'im! **John Pratt** b.1905

‘I was caned for not having learnt a hymn!’

There was a lot of rote learning and if you didn't get it right, if you didn't learn it, you sometimes got the cane. I remember getting the cane for not having learned a hymn in the length of time we'd been given to learn it. **George Handley** b.1937

Yes, it was fairly tough [boarding at Sedbergh School]. The cold baths in the morning, fagging, beatings by prefects, by housemasters and by headmasters. It was part of the discipline system. You went up to the bathroom and you leant over the bath and he had a cane that he used… well all prefects were allowed to do beating, and you'd get six of the best on the bottom and sometimes there was three of them involved and they just followed one after the other… Oh, you could get done for having your hands in your pockets, and caught out of bounds, and probably for something to do with the cleaning of your boots. **David Hutchinson** b.1920

I went to Cowgill School and we had a school mistress, she was built like a brick shithouse, six foot tall, and oh, she was horrendous! I went to school in clogs, I got many a hiding off her, she wanted you in slippers. I'd tell me dad and he'd say 'I went to school in clogs, you'll go to school in clogs'. I got many a caning for that, she was a terror… She used to live at Deeside House [Cowgill], she had an autocycle and she used to go back for her dinner. There was a pack on the back with a big belt, she sent you out for that, then she'd pull your jacket up, lean you over desk and lay into you. One occasion at dinnertime a girl called Mary Ellis, from Acre, she said 'we'll get out of school half an hour early' and she put the clock on. But immediately the teacher came back in she knew, and she asked 'who's put clock on?' and nobody answered. I think at that time there'd be over thirty pupils, she lined the lot up and caned every one. She made sure she got right 'un! She was a GI bride, she married a Yankee at the end of the war. **Alan Mattinson** b.1934

We didn't need a lot of discipline. You just respected people, which was totally different then. Discipline was there if it was necessary but we were more scared of our own father and mother, who were not bad to us, but you just did not cause problems if you could help it, and we would be more worried that the teacher would tell our parents who would then chastise us far more than what smacking us or anything like that might have done at that time. Not that I think it's wrong. I still believe that a slap at the right time's a good thing. **Kenneth Cragg** b.1936

'Tig…skipping…marbles…hopscotch'

Well, somebody would stand up agin a wall an' you would go an' touch them an' then they would run an' try an' catch you. Was it tig? An' then yer 'ad skippin'… you would 'ave a big rope an' they would put one at each end, an' turn it, an' then yer would all run in an' all jump together, an' that would be when yer say 'All in together boys, this fine weather boys'. Then there would be a little bit more and then 'All fall out!' an' you would all 'ave t' run out! An' then you'd have skippin' jus' on yer own wi' skippin' ropes, an' then there was a competition where they tried to see who could skip the most in a minute, an' they would time them an' see 'ow many skips they could make – an' it was a tremendous quantity when they did it really fast! And they even went down to Sedbergh an' they 'ad a competition there. That was part of this sports do, this skippin', an' there were some in Dent, by jove, that were absolutely terrific! The skips they could make! They went so fast! **Cissy Middleton** b.1914

> *That was our football – bladders at pig-killing time*

Marbles was a great idea. But t' trouble was, somebody finished up with all the marbles and then you'd to buy them off him and start all over again! **Willie Whitwell** b.1914

A football was out of this world! All it was was a sack, the old type of sack wrapped up with hairy string, as we used to call it, and that was t' football. [If it was wet] it used t' weigh about half a stone! It never came off the ground, really! Or we used to get about three of those bladders at pig-killing time! But it only used to last about ten minutes, of course, because [it hit] a clog! It was blown up and when it got burst they used to just finish up in the corner of the yard, and the smell of them by the end of the month! **Bob Turner** b.1933

If it was wet we used to play hopscotch in the cloakrooms… At one time we did have a hockey team, that would be when I was about twelve years old. We had quite a good team; we used to go to Sedbergh and play the team down there. I used to play goalie or the right wing. **Betty Hartley** b.1913

Oh, we had a wonderful teacher in the twenties, Mr Teer. When Mr Teer came he wanted us to play a game. Well of course the playgrounds were too rough to play games like tennis or cricket, so he found out there's a game called stoolball in which the wicket was on a pole and there was a white square, so if the bowler could hit the square you were out. And you had a bat that was similar to a table tennis bat only heavier. So that was marvellous. All the positions were just as they were in French cricket. **Marjorie Middleton** b.1913

Every day in the winter terms, if a boy wasn't put down to play football [at Sedbergh School] one of the prefects would put a notice up on the house noticeboard saying the exercise run for today is this or that. And there were a number of accepted routes which we got to know and had to follow. On a whole school day they were about three and a half miles long, but on a half holiday they could be seven, eight, or even more miles occasionally. And everybody was expected to go on that exercise if they weren't down for a set game. The only other exceptions were if you were playing squash or fives. But otherwise in the summer term of course we had great freedom to go just as far as our legs would carry us. There weren't quite the same number of set games; there was cricket every day but if you were lucky and could persuade a house prefect not to put your name down to play cricket, then you could go off for the whole afternoon. **Ingram Cleasby** b.1920

I can't ever remember missing a day of school, I mean there was so much t' do. There were only the two classes. The room was just split by a big glass and wood

❛*When Cowgill school closed the children had to go to Dent, and hated it!* ❜ partition but on cold days the partition was open because there was only one means of heating and that was a huge coke stove that was in the middle of the floor. So the elder of the boys, they used to be given the job of going out to the coke heap, which was in the corner, and filling the bucket up, bringing it in, and of course the teacher used to feed the stove. But when the wind was in the wrong direction it used t' blow back down the flue, and of course it used to fill the classroom with fumes! Everybody was sent home then! We used to pray for the wind to come over the fell! **Bob Turner** b.1933

No school dinners!

We allus had t' take a basket o' food wi' us because there was no dinners made then but we used to 'ave a basket wi' a lid on, o'er each side, an' it was packed wi' sandwiches, probably only bread and jam! But when it came t' dinner time there was a huge fire in one o' the main rooms an' we jus' used t' sit round an' eat our sandwiches. There was no cups o' tea, nothin' like that, but if we wanted a drink we went out in t' playground an' there was a stand tap an' we jus' used t' put our 'eads under t' tap an' have a drink o' water an' that was what we got. **Cissy Middleton** b.1914

We had a jigger and it was on a fire. A right big kettle – you know, like a straight up round big kettle with a tap at t' bottom, and a lid at t' top. You filled it wi' water. Yes, a big iron urn. We allus called it a jigger. And we boiled that and then they all brought cocoa or tea, whichever they wanted, and you just brewed it in the pot. They brought their own dinner with 'em. They're spoiled nowadays. **Mary Ellison** b.1909

Happy days! But one by one the smaller schools were closed, and with them went much of the vitality they had brought to their local communities.

Before Sue [daughter] was born, I taught at Cowgill school for a time. Miss Wilkinson was the teacher and I went as assistant. There must have been as many as thirty children I think, at one time, because I had the infants in the little room until Susan came along and I left. I stayed at home until Sue was about five or six and then I went back to Cowgill school for a time. In fact I was Head at Cowgill from 1964 to 1967 when it closed. Cowgill school closed under me. And I went with the children on to Dent, but the Cowgill children hated it. They used to come crying to me at school – but they adapted in the end. **Betty Harper** b.1920

CHAPTER 3

Land and labour

Farm sizes and types – The workforce –
Walling – Hiring fairs

Changes in farming practices may have come late to the dales but when they arrived they overturned a way of life that had endured for generations. Interviewees recalling their memories of conditions in the 1920s and particularly the agricultural depression of the 1930s speak of the hardship many farming folk endured. Nevertheless, as the twentieth century progressed new technology gradually helped to improve working conditions as mowing machines did the work of scythes and early milking machines, powered by generators, saved the labour of hand milking. The occasional motor vehicle was making its appearance, too, but in general horses were still relied on for moving goods and people.

Although the size of farms varied, the typical upland farm in the dales was small by modern standards. Many were rented, some were owned outright. Until sometime after the Second World War the income generally came from mixed farming, principally sheep and cows, with poultry and pigs providing much-needed food as well as extra cash.

Our memories of these times fill the next five chapters, starting with land and labour before focusing in turn on cattle, sheep, pigs and poultry, and haytiming.

Farm sizes and types

We moved into Howgill when I was six years old, 1920 I think it was, and we farmed there for twenty six years. In those days in the valley, Howgill and Firbank, there were thirty six farms. There's eighteen now, just half. The small farms have been bought up by the larger ones and the farmhouses have been made into private houses [separated from the land]. **Willie Whitwell** b.1914

Dent farms were small farms but in those days if you just worked them yourself you could make a living, a modest living, but people didn't expect a high standard of living. We didn't have all these gadgets that we have now, televisions and goodness knows what! We just lived in the old-fashioned way and so making a living wasn't so difficult. **Helga Frankland** b.1920

We came to farm in Oaks at Marthwaite, we had thirty nine acres and there were five farms mostly round the forty acre mark. We had six thousand hens, eight cows, and we supplied Libby McNeill & Libby at Milnthorpe with milk for the tinning process. **Leslie Robinson** b.1930

> *The nearest to a machine in our house was a sewing machine*

We were on a rented farm, that's all my father did. It was enough because we had twenty odd cattle, eighty to a hundred sheep. We sold milk right through to the bitter end, no milking machine. The nearest to a machine in our house was a sewing machine with pedals! **Dick Harrison** b.1934

Mr Burra was the Lord of the Manor of Dent and he lived at Gate. He was selling up and [my brother] Raven persuaded my mother to buy several of his farms, and indeed the common rights. So he became the Lord of the Manor of Frostrow. I am now the Lady of the Manor of Frostrow because my mother left them to us. **Helga Frankland** b.1920

Sir Albert Braithwaite, he owned a lot of properties, he owned Whernside Manor, that's where he used to come in the shooting season, he owned a load of farms. Him and Raven Frankland between them probably owned the dale. And Burras at Gate Manor, they were another of the big landowners. My dad, he would only milk seven or eight cows and carry about forty to fifty sheep up on the fell. And hens, he used to sell eggs for hatching. **Alan Mattinson** b.1934

I think it was about 1680 when one of my ancestors bought it [High Bargh, Dent] and it's stayed in our family all the time after that. Of course this was before the enclosures, and it set off with about fourteen acres of meadow land and nine acres of pasture land and then what is now the allotments was of course then common land so the cattle and sheep would go up there [in summer]… We had twenty four acres of meadow land and twenty five of pasture land and then we had two allotments, one went up Rise Hill, it was forty acres, then we crossed Langstone Fell an' we had one went down towards Garsdale and that was another forty acres. **Kenneth Cragg** b.1936

The allotments are parcels of fell land used for rough grazing. In Dentdale this top land had been enclosed in the mid nineteenth century, when each farm was allotted a share in proportion to its size. In the Sedbergh area, however, the hills were never fenced, so grazing rights on the Howgills continued to be organised by committees of local farmers, as they are to this day. (See Chapter 5 on sheep farming).

[My parents] did mixed farming [at Butterpots, Deepdale], same as it is now really. There's forty acres in-bye and about a hundred and twenty acres fell land. I can remember them milking eight, nine or ten cows, then there was the followers [calves]. And there was Swaddells [Swaledale sheep] yes, a hundred and twenty breeding ewes. **Miley Taylor** b.1923

While [my husband] was away [at war] auntie and I were offered Cage Farm. The Underley Estate [which included several farms in Dentdale] was breaking up, you see, and they offered the tenants the first chance, so my dad said before he died, 'If it's ever to sell, buy it!'. Well it was to sell and my husband was away in North Africa, nobody to ask, so we took the plunge and we raised enough money and we just paid twelve hundred pounds and that was for twenty eight acres of exceptionally good land. **Betty Hartley** b.1913

Me father took up the farming of the Greenwell farm two years after he retired because it was the homestead of his parents and his grandparents. He did buy Far Helks about 1924, so as to be two farms together, to make 'em a bit bigger. And when me wife and I got married in 1933 we lived in the Far Helks farmhouse. But when me father died we come down here [to Greenwell] about three years after. And I've carried on farming here since, and me son decided he would farm an' all. That's how it is, we're farming under G C Ellison & Son. I purchased Doubie Croft to make it a bit bigger still, and then as things are today that isn't enough. We rent two fields off the Dent Grammar School charity. **George Ellison** b.1908

> *The tenant farmer is the salt of this country!*

It's a job in Dent getting hold o' land. Everybody's wantin', it isn't a case of greedy folk or owt like that but everybody's wantin' extra land. 'Cause I'm farmin' stock,

I've bin in it all me life an' I like me sheep, I'm sixty-six now an' whether, 'ow long, I'm still as keen as mustard wi' me sheep. There ain't as much money in it now, but the tenant farmer is the salt of this country! The tenant farmer knows what 'e 'as t' mek t' live! **Reg Charnley** b.1942

Coat Faw was in t' Middleton family about seventy year, rented. [The landlords were] Lady Henry and Lord Henry Bentinck. They came round at shooting times when they were residing at Dee Side [their hunting lodge in Cowgill]. They'd come round visiting tenants, to ask 'em if they were comfortable. They were very good landlords. She had lovely hair, yellow-coloured hair, and she sat side-saddle on t' horse. **Bessie Mason** b.1911

When agricultural depression hit, as it did in the 1930s, this kind of subsistence farming led to real hardship and poverty.

I've always felt really that the hard-working stock of this area has never been fully appreciated, because it must still be inbred in these people, and some of them that are living to be as old as I am now, I know they will have lived through that very, very hard time when they were children – the tenant farmers especially. The ones that owned their own farms were definitely better off. They generally had a pig, and I think that probably provided them with what meat they got during the winter, but I think it was fed on anything they could find: potato peelings or whatever…

❝ Children never had new clothes, always cut-down things from relatives ❞

Some of them were desperately poor.
They only really had any income twice a year, and that was very limited. They had nothing to sell as such: no stock, until the lambs were big enough to sell in the late summer, and the young calves were big enough to be sold on in the autumn to go to other places to winter because they often had so little hay grass in the dales that they couldn't keep the young stock. They were obliged to sell them in the autumn to keep their nucleus stock over the winter. That was what the hay was used for. And they literally hadn't the money to buy proven for them…

The first lot of income was when they sheared the sheep, which would be about June. But if they were tenant farmers that money had to go to pay their rent so that wasn't really available for the families, so the only money they had really coming in was the end of the summer when the young livestock was sold, and then of course they needed the money to provide for the winter, for both the families and their stock. I don't think anybody really realises now what real poverty is. Some of the children never had new clothes; they were always things that were cut down from relatives, the girls especially – I think the boys did a bit better. And anything that was knitted, if the wool was recyclable it was recycled. And that struck me very much because of the two halves of my family, where one half had everything that anybody could want and the other half… I saw this other side of life altogether. That was why so many emigrated to New Zealand where a lot of them are now very wealthy. Families used to come round and visit my mother and father, half-cousins and cousins of my father's that he'd known as a boy, that had gone out there on these schemes, these ten pound or something schemes, and they started with a cow selling a bit of milk to the nearest village, then the village had grown to be a town and the town had grown to be a city and he'd bought a field when he could, and ended up a very wealthy man. It was lovely to see them really but it had never gone to their heads, they were still the basic Dales people. **Jean Donald** b.1921

The workforce

All the bigger farms would have had a man and probably a girl as well in service to help, and there was no feeling that this was in any way *infra dig*, it was the only and natural outlet, for small farms couldn't support a number of sons and daughters, they had to go out to service to find work to do and then they would get married and have a farm of their own eventually, if they were lucky. I have some very happy memories of them, we were very devoted to some of the farm servants. **Ingram Cleasby** b.1920

Ingram got a taste of what it was like to be a farm labourer just after he'd left school.

I'd enlisted in the first week of the war but wasn't called up immediately, in fact kept waiting and waiting for my papers and in the end spent several months working on a local farm, filling in the time, which was a very happy experience. This was The Oaks, at Marthwaite. It was a very small farm and very traditional in that we had a small dairy herd of, I think, probably seven or eight cows and a little bit of arable and a small flock of sheep and the pig, which was duly killed in my honour and which we proceeded to consume for the next few months in various forms, and that in itself was

> *All paraffin lamps, no hot water except it was boiled in a kettle*

quite an education. This was a family farm and the farmer, he and his wife just had small children. I think he had been helped by his brother, but then the brother was called up and when I heard that he was in real difficulties I offered to come and help him for a time, which he was very pleased to agree to, and they provided me with my board and lodging. That also was great experience because it was a very primitive farm indeed, paraffin lamps, no hot water except it was boiled in a kettle. **Ingram Cleasby** b.1920

Helga Frankland's grandfather bought a farm in Ravenstonedale in 1909, added another to it the following year and went on to acquire more. Since both he and his son, Helga's father, worked as academic scientists, they needed to employ others to work their land.

We had men working on the farm who we liked and respected very much and they, well, one of them, the man [George Fothergill] who was headman for most of my childhood and indeed right through the war and until we gave up farming, he practically brought us up so far as the farming side and a lot of the outdoor life was concerned. **Helga Frankland** b.1920

Workers on larger farms such as this were lucky enough to have permanent jobs. Many farmhands, though, were hired for six months at a time. It was usual for them to get board and lodging, which helped to make up for their low wages.

The first job I had I went to a small farm, Rawridding [Dentdale], Tommy Staveley [paid me] eight pounds for six months. I started work at six o'clock in the morning and we never finished before seven o'clock at night, this was seven days

❝ I was 'hurled', held, or bonded like a slave ❞

a week except on Saturday and Sunday we had a treat, we finished work about six o'clock. That was a treat. I lived in, I had eight pounds and my keep. We were well fed. It was mixed farming, milking, sheep farming and rearing, the whole thing. That was the first job I had when I left school. **Albert Fothergill** b.1923

I worked at home the first year after I left school. Then I went to work at Stonehouse Farm [Cowgill], that would be for Sir Albert Braithwaite. I was working under a hind, he was a farmhand, and I was under him even. **Alan Mattinson** b.1934

I was fourteen and just out of school and me dad and mum couldn't keep me. Me dad, he were looking out for a place. You know, he couldn't find any, there was nowhere… I didn't want to go on to a farm but I had no option. Me dad just went across to [an outlying Dentdale farm]. It's a wild place. And [the farmer] come across and they talked about one thing and another and mentioned this amount o' money and – they didn't ask me anything about it – and me dad says, 'You're going across there to work'. I said, 'Oh aye', and that was it, twenty pound for twenty six weeks. An' no mention of time, how well I worked or owt. But I knew what I'd to do to work, 'cos I knew what he were like. He were a slave driver, my word! And he gave me a shilling into me palm o' me hand and shook me hand. And that meant that I was 'hurled', I was held, or bonded like a slave. And if I'd gone, walked out on 'im in a tiff or anything like that, nobody else would have hired me. So that was t' conditions you were hired under them days. **Fred Taylor** b.1927

My older brother was at home and there wasn't enough work for me as well, so I went out… I lived in [at Quernmore] and the reason I packed up in the end, the family were staunch Methodists and I'd been brought up Church of England, and one day I used some bad language and the boss was not very pleased, and I said 'Well I'm afraid I just can't live under this environment, I'm going home'. And he said 'Oh you can't without your parents' permission'. An' I said 'Oh can't I?', so I just got on my bike and I came home. That was the end of that job. My father asked why I'd come home and I told him, but I also said they were employing boys to do men's work. I was asked to carry sixteen-stone bags of wheat 'cos in them days it used to come in two-hundredweight bags. We'd to carry them up some steps and hang them over a beam. I fell with the bag and Mr Fox says 'Come on, get up, pick it up' and I cursed 'im because I said I couldn't, I wasn't strong enough, I was only fifteen. I was pretty strong, I could lift hundredweight bags quite easy but not this two-hundredweight bag – and I told him what to do with his bag o' wheat…

> *I'd never used a bath in my life*

It was very, very hard. You started at six in a morning, you finished at six at night, for six days. Sunday you worked until ten o'clock, then you had to go to chapel. After chapel you had lunch and you'd three hours off. Then you'd to start milking again Sunday night, and I got every fourth weekend off to go home. That was just regular conditions then. But I was well fed. Mrs Fox was a wonderful cook. I'd a good home as regards inside the house. I remember having to use her bath, having a bath and got told off. I hadn't cleaned it out, not knowing that you had to, and, well there was this black line round it 'cos I would naturally not be very clean having worked out on the farm. I'd never used a bath in my life. **Kenneth Cragg** b. 1936

Walling

One of the most distinctive features of the dales landscape is the network of dry stone walls dividing field from field. Maintaining them and 'gapping up' was always a labour-intensive job for farmers. Walling without mortar is no easy task, especially when the ground is rough and steep. A good waller was always in demand, and the best of them took a great pride in their craft.

It's a skill an' it's either in yer or it's not in yer to do it. Dent stone is the finest walling stone there is. Yer allus knit yer stones tight t' the next one, a tight joint, because if yer don't, when it freezes it lifts up and drops it when it thaws out. The middle wants t' be an inch higher, an yer keep yer nose up so it keeps wattershaken, watterkest, keeps the water out. When yer put a wall up yer stand back and 'ave a look at it. If yer see any faults yer think 'Oh, should never 'ave put that stone in there', or 'I 'aven't med a bad job o' that!'. **Reg Charnley** b.1942

Tom Sedgwick remembers his father telling him about the building of the Dent allotment walls high on the fells in the 1860s, and how the workers fed themselves on what the Scots called 'brose'.

They used to take a bag of meal. They'd have some in their bag and they used to eat meal, me father said, and drink at beck. Just oatmeal, as it is. **Tom Sedgwick** b.1917

Hiring fairs

If men and young lads weren't hired through a private deal they could offer their labour at one of the hiring fairs. These were held every six months at Martinmas [November] and Whitsuntide in Sedbergh and Kendal.

The only thing they looked for was if you could milk, and mow with a scythe. And what I felt sorry about, at t' end of Saturday night, after t' hirings, there was these poor lads that was weaklings, they were all left without jobs. And they might have been quite good up here wi' brains, but you see they wanted somebody with t' strength. And they used to ask which hand you were, if you were left-handed or right-handed, and they used to feel at your muscles. It was degrading really. I mean t' farmer had to have somebody like that, hadn't he? **Fred Taylor** b.1927

'Some loose-end men weren't worth paying with washers!'

You generally went to Kendal and hired somebody at hirings… We had a lad for six years lived at Nun House [Deepdale], he came to us every day, he came after he'd milked at home, stopped with us through day for t' week, he didn't come on a Sunday, just for six days. That's all help we had most of time. Grand lad was Jack, he came when he left school until he was twenty one… [The pay] wasn't so much, at first it was only into teens for six month, you paid 'em for six months, you see. Just the way everything was. **Mary Ellison** b.1909

A lot of farmers used to have to hire an Irishman for the month [at haytime]. As all the work was to do by hand you needed more people, and thousands of men used to come over from Ireland for a month for the haymaking season here. **Betty Hartley** b.1913

Just before haytime there was quite a lot of Irishmen used to come in and they were nearly all Catholics, and they used to walk to church at Bentham, it'll be seventeen or eighteen miles [from Dent]. They couldn't afford to pay 'em two months, and if hay wasn't got in they went. **Miley Taylor** b.1923

There used to be men come round, what did they call 'em – loose-end men – and they would hire theirselves for a week or a day or two, and if they weren't in good condition they weren't much good at first, but when they got well fed up they mended. You never 'ad separate tables, they were made like one o' t' family. But some men weren't worth paying wi' washers, you see, so they 'ad to go! **Bessie Mason** b.1911

If you couldn't milk and you couldn't mow with a scythe you were no good to anyone. But that's t' way it was. **Fred Taylor** b.1927

CHAPTER 4

Cattle

Types of herds – Milking and milk rounds –
Cows to the customers – Butter and cheese –
Milk collection and the Marketing Board –
Modernisation...and decline – Beef rearing –
Marketing, auction marts and 'luck' –
Slaughtering

Before the Second World War most dales farms had at least a few cows. The size of milking herds varied. Some farms might have as many as sixty but the majority kept fewer than a dozen. The recollections in this chapter cover changing fashions in types of herd, the switch from milk to beef production – and some unconventional slaughtering practices.

Types of herds

We had fifteen cows, we'd quite a big herd in Dent with fifteen. A lot had seven or eight cows, they were all milked by hand. **Kenneth Cragg** b.1936

We didn't keep a lot o' cattle, probably just into the teens. We used to rear 'em as calves and keep 'em probably one summer or so, and make butter of the milk, and then when they calved a second time we'd probably sell 'em 'cos we had some more following up every year to fill their places. **John Pratt** b.1905

Our business in those days was buying heifer calves from lowland farmers, bringing 'em up and selling 'em new-calved, to go to the near towns – Sedbergh, Kendal, Liverpool and things like that… At Marthwaite we would have about twenty, we might get up to twenty five. **Myles Jackson** b.1928

The dairy cows were mainly of one breed, a type Ingram Cleasby's grandfather had helped to improve back in the mid nineteenth century. His grandfather died in 1895.

By this time cattle breeding had become quite a specialised and sophisticated business and he certainly bred pedigree cattle, which was probably unusual when he began but was becoming the thing. They were called Northern Dairy Shorthorns. **Ingram Cleasby** b.1920

Dairy Shorthorns, I loved them. Never liked it once we changed to t' others. I loved animals and I made pets of 'em all. I'd go down to the shippon at bedtime and they'd all stand up and look at me and, it was funny, I used to tickle their horns. **Mary Ellison** b.1909

We were one of the first in the valley to change over to the Friesians. Produced more milk off the same acreage so therefore we didn't have to buy more land, we just produced more milk. **Kenneth Cragg** b.1936

Milking and milk rounds

In the days before milking machines labourers and family members alike were expected to be able to milk by hand. For anyone not used to it, hand milking could be a tough learning experience.

I can't remember when I started but I did learn to milk. I was never interested or good at it 'cos the midges would bite and half of the time you were only milking with one hand 'cos the other was scratting for midges! **Dick Harrison** b.1934

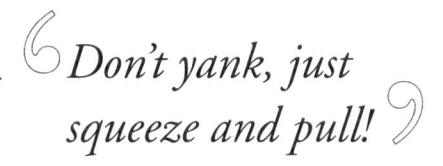

"Don't yank, just squeeze and pull!"

The cows during the winter were kept indoors in a shippon and I was expected to start milking immediately, which was something I had very little experience of, and to milk three or four cows when your hands are not accustomed to it is quite demanding. I can remember it was very, very cold at that time, bitter frosts, and getting up at six o'clock in the morning in the dark and making one's way across the yard to the shippon, which was lit by a paraffin lamp, one was very pleased to snuggle down beside one's cow because she was nice and warm. The great point then, would she give up her milk? But eventually I got into the way of it and could milk my three or four cows fairly well, but my hands for months afterwards were still swollen from the unaccustomed exercise. **Ingram Cleasby** b.1920

Bob Turner learnt to milk by helping his neighbour Dick Middleton with his herd of eighteen cows.

As a boy I was given the cow's tail to hold so that it didn't whip round Dick's ear'ole, and then it used t' shoot a jet of milk straight at you! They didn't hang about! Just give you a bucket and a three-legged coppet [stool] and say, 'Right', you know, 'just lean against it with yer head and don't yank, just squeeze and pull'! And it was surprising how quick you learnt! **Bob Turner** b.1933

Me mother wouldn't let me milk. She said if you got a husband that went out drinking you'd 'ave to do it yerself, and she wasn't going to 'ave me doing that! **Bessie Mason** b.1911

I think me dad would have over twenty at one time but they 'ad t' be scattered out in different barns, some would be quite a distance away, there was only so many could be fitted into a big barn. Therefore they milked at home an' then they 'ad t' go out wi' their back-can an' milk at these out-places, an' bring this milk back in their back-can on their shoulders, you know, straps, that's 'ow it fitted, an' they'd 'ave t' go probably nearly one an' a half miles, way out at high side, to fetch it… This was in winter. But after that we put a new shippon up an' got them all under one roof, which made it a lot better. **Cissy Middleton** b.1914

Way back before the war and during the war, because then milk got partly rationed, I think I counted about eleven different farms that hawked milk round Sedbergh. Some of them had 'orses and floats, some of them even had bikes with bottles on 'andlebars, and they had old carts and what not. All farms within about, oh, a mile of Sedbergh and of course in them days most farms could be anywhere from thirty-odd acres towards a hundred, so to sell your milk directly and draw money for it, it was revenue into your hand. And a number of the schoolchildren used to go out and 'elp these fellows to take their milk out. Some of 'em used to go round with jugs, some of 'em had bottles, but I remember at the British School when I was there they started the free milk [for schools] in the little gill bottle. **Leslie Robinson** b.1930

> *We sold milk in little cans looped on either side of the bike*

Our milk was delivered… we had Alderson's, they were up Howgill Lane, that farm. Peggy used to deliver the milk in a cart and horse and the horse stopped at our house, Peggy brought a big can, my mother went to the door with a jug, and that's how the milk came. **Jean Rochford** b.c1927

We had a cooler for the milk, we sold milk from [Garsdale Hall] to a few different places. We took them in little cans – are they aluminium? – little light cans… Yes, on a bike up as far as Bainbridge Road we used to go. Some would hold maybe a pint, some half a pint. They had handles on and a lid, we looped them either side of the bike. Yes, every day. And then eventually we sold milk to the school in those little bottles. I know when we got them back we had to rinse them all out with water and then wash them and then just set them all up and pour boiling water in to sterilise them. **Mary Cowperthwaite** b.1924

Len Nelson was just coming home from his milk round. There'd just been a show in Scarrs field and so his float was lovely, cleaned up, painted, the harness shone and all the cans in the back they shone brightly so that he was going in for a prize at the show… Armisteads from Borret were coming home from their milk round and they too had been in the show so their milk float was beautifully painted. In the town itself there were other milk people because we had in total some seven milkmen used to come round delivering milk. There were the Sedgwicks from Lockbank, there was Aldersons from The Hill up Joss Lane, there was Winns from Castle Haw, there was Harpers from Benson Bank and there was Dixons from the Green. So all these horses were coming in. They didn't have patches where one man had one road, they all followed one another round. The horses actually knew where the clients were better than the drivers did and some of t' ladies used to come out with their jugs to collect their supply of milk and some of the men used to come out and collect the supplies left by the horses! So there were good rose trees growing in most of the roads! **David Hutchinson** b.1920

Cows to the customers

A number of dales families came up with their own answer to the milk distribution problem. They took the cows to the consumers.

My grandparents came to live in Dent. They were dales people but, like so many families, they had lived in Liverpool. Well in Liverpool they had what they call the milk house. It was in fact a farm, they kept cows, they had fields down behind the Botanic Gardens and a farm yard, cow sheds and things, and they did five milk rounds with ponies and floats. So it must have been a great harnessing up in the morning to get all these floats ready for off. The stock I think came down from the dales by train. About sixty cows, something like that. It must have been before the First World War they moved down there. **Hazel Haygarth** b.1922

Me parents were cow keepers and dairy people in Liverpool. Me father come back to Dent on account of me mother not being so well after 'aving been twenty six years in the cowkeeping business and that was in 1920. And I came back then, I was between eleven and twelve years old. **George Ellison** b.1908

“We bartered butter for shopping. No money changed hands”

Butter and cheese

Before we sold milk we made butter. Edmondsons used to have a shop on Main Street [Sedbergh] and they used to buy butter. I can still see the big square wooden butter boxes and the butter pats that they used to make it square, with patterns on. **Dick Harrison** b.1934

That was Thursday's job, mekin' butter. This massive churn, a hand operated churn, and then as t' butter was med I used to knock it up into pieces wi' 'scotch hands', into pounds. And then a big basket used to go down to Dent village with t' butter to Batty's shop, and then fetch t' shopping back. And there was no money, there wasn't a lot of money changed hands. But the amount of butter that I took down, I fetched t' value of shopping back. It was like barter. Well it's a good way really isn't it? No money involved. **Fred Taylor** b.1927

They used to make butter, the ladies. I can remember turning the end-over-end churn me'self. It was hard work. Then you had the separator, which separated the cream from the milk, or the lead – poured it into the lead, let it stand and then you let the milk out. That was the blue milk, and the cream stood on the lead and you just wiped it off. **Miley Taylor** b.1923

An' then of course you saved all yer cream an' put it into another big pot, that went down in to yer cellar, to keep cool an' nice 'cos it 'ad t' stay for a week, 'cos you only churned once a week. An' of course it 'ad t' get ripe. An' then night before you would probably bring it up an' jus' leave it in yer livin' room so that it got that chill from it. Churn used t' come an' be set in front o' t' fireplace, that was for wintertime. In summertime it was taken right down in t' cellar where it was really cool, it was like under t' ground an' it was all flagged an' there would be 'oles in these big flag stones if yer wanted t' put a lead in an' run yer milk out. It was a cold job, was makin' butter, 'cos yer'd t' keep yer 'ands cold fer work, but then we got that we didn' use our 'ands at all, got it that yer never touched butter at all with me 'ands in t' finish 'cos we learned the proper way t' make it…

Meself and two other sisters, we all three of us went to learn 'ow to make butter properly. Leeds University came and they took t' old Grammar School building in Dent [to run classes] because butter many a time wasn't fit to eat. You know, they didn't get the buttermilk out, you would see butter a bit on t' bitter side, and streaky, light and dark. I have me certificate in t' kitchen window there… We had a fourteen days course to make this butter. And it was perfect, was t' butter. Metcalfes in Sedbergh paid tuppence a pound more for my butter! An' when I was seventeen I entered for Lunesdale Show. Well do you know, I carried t' first prize off! Out of all these old women that used to always do this butter and oh, I think it upset 'em, they couldn't get over the fact that this young lass of seventeen beat 'em! **Cissy Middleton** b.1914

> *'It was a feast for the gods, home-made bread, home-made Wensleydale cheese, home-made butter'*

It would be 1930s when milk started being collected, maybe… We separated it to make butter and we fed t' skimmed milk to t' pigs and t' calves. Me mother used to mek cheese in summer. Dinsdales used to come round with a hoss and a lorry, two hosses sometimes, and they'd bring t' shopping in t' butter box, and then put t' butter into t' box and tek it. Dinsdale lived at Dent, in t' Stores, and he would sell from his shop. And then he would have his ports [outlets] – he would maybe tek some on t' train, Dent station. **Jim Middleton** b.1913

It was a feast for the gods was home-baked bread, homemade cheese, Wensleydale cheese, with homemade butter. It was absolutely wonderful! You didn't know it at the time but… The cheese, of course, had to be matured in the dairy. It was wrapped with muslin, it had to be turned over regularly, but it tasted wonderful! **Betty Harper** b.1920

Milk collection and the Marketing Board

In Dentdale, Frank Dinsdale was the first to organise regular collections of milk. He had a farm and he had the shop, Dinsdale's Stores in the village, and he had this small cheese factory down at the back of the stores. He got milk from the farms and he supplied each farm with a gallon measure, I remember me dad getting one. And then he started at t' top o' Deepdale and Jack Middleton had his horse and trap with Blossom in, and he'd two big seventeen-gallon cans and he come down and he stopped at every farm that had any surplus milk and fetched it down to Dent and made cheese of it there. And that was before the Milk Marketing Board was formed I think in 1933. **Fred Taylor** b.1927

> *My father was getting sixpence a gallon and he thought he'd struck a fortune!*

It was a great saviour to these people. I can remember all the farmers in Deepdale meeting in this yard [Butterpots] discussing selling milk to Frank Dinsdsale in Dent, and how they would get it there, who would take it down. Mr Dinsdale bought it and then the Milk Marketing Board took it up. You got a guaranteed price for your milk. **Miley Taylor** b.1923

When me father started selling milk about 1928 up at Cote Faw [Cowgill] 'e was getting sixpence a gallon an' 'e thought 'e 'ad struck a fortune! He used to go to Dinsdale's at Dent. **Jack Middleton** b.1921

The Milk Marketing Board was set up in 1933 to ensure that all milk produced on farms was hygienic, collected and sold at a controlled price.

It was the first time farmers in Dent had been better off. Frank Dinsdale really set us all off producing milk. At first we were producing what we called a kit a day, a kit was twelve gallon in those days which was your milk churn size, and we were selling about twelve gallons a day, and when we got finished in the 1950s we would be sending about thirty gallons a day. We'd two full kits and a half at the time of year when the cows were milking best. I remember in 1948 we were getting four shillings a gallon for the milk. **Kenneth Cragg** b.1936

It was yer livelihood, sellin' yer milk! I mean t' Milk Marketing Board used t' send you your cheque every month an' it was a boon was that because you knew it come in. It was a big pity when it stopped. **Cissy Middleton** b.1914

"No purification system, you just yanked it through your teeth and picked all the germs out"

Modernisation – and decline

In the late fifties we thought that the Milk Marketing Board was trying to find ways of getting rid, there was too many little dairy farms, and they came along to test the water that we used, 'cos we had our own water supply came out of Thackthwaite beck. No [purification system], just that you yanked it through your teeth and picked all the little germs out, but we drank it as the family, and my mother's ninety now and it never did her any harm. It was used for washing the utensils, boiled of course, and these people [the Board] came along and took a sample and they said it wasn't fit to use even when it was boiled, so they stopped us selling milk. And that was a big blow. **Kenneth Cragg** b.1936

Mother and father were always of the view that it was the milk cheque that was the be all and end all, and the thing that always terrified them was if a letter came that there would be some sort of inspection. They then had to pretend they were milking in the six-cow byre rather than the twenty-cow byre. They were terrified that the shippon would be condemned for milk, which it should have been and would have been later on, but we never died of it. It was only once that a pup was found swimming in the milk kit, as I recall. **Kevin Lancaster** b.1959

Outsiders? They're nobbut a damned nuisance, that's all. **Tom Sedgwick** b.1917

We used to cool our milk in t' beck, put it into a kit and put it into t' stream. And then you see t' regulations altered and we had to get a cooler. And then these old scrap fellers used to come round buying these old coolers when they went out of fashion. **Jim Middleton** b.1913

I never had a milking machine here, no, it was all done by hand till, I forget the date – 1970s. But the first thing to happen, the water wasn't fit, they said, they wanted people out. The water wasn't fit to wash the utensils in but it was fit enough for us to drink! Gave up the milking herd, so yeah, I'm on dried milk now! **Miley Taylor** b.1923

I remember going to Kendal and ordering me tractor and a milking machine t' same day. I got t' milking machine going – we sweat harder milking with that thing than what we did wi' t' hand. It was one of these portable things. We thought we'd be able to tek it into t' shippon in t' back o' transport box but it didn't prove a success, didn't that. So we put it stationary… But it did, and that was it. **Jim Middleton** b.1913

For many small farmers the new hygiene regulations meant the end of milk production, and gradually fewer milk kits were to be seen waiting on stands by the roadside for collection by the milk lorries. The remaining dairy farmers were generally the larger producers who benefited from improved facilities.

We were supplying the Milk Board in Kendal, they had a milk factory then at Kendal, so one of the Board came to see us, he said 'Associated Dairies are wanting bulk milk in Leeds so would you be interested in putting a bulk tank in?'. So life was going to be a lot easier so we put a bulk tank in for two hundred and fifty gallons and the ASDA, Associated Dairies, picked our milk up in a morning, it never was later than nine o'clock, and they boasted it was on the doorstep in Leeds the following morning. So from there till the late seventies we were producing milk and supplying Associated Dairies. **Leslie Robinson** b.1930

The milk only went once a day. It was stored, it was put through the cooler and went out in the morning so that the milk van, wagon as it was, used to pick it up round about nine o'clock. I know we always used to miss it because we'd gone t' school. They were twelve-gallon milk kits as they were known, so they used to get wheeled down on edge, just rolled round, hand to hand, and then lifted with a knee, but I couldn't… they were far too heavy. **Bob Turner** b.1933

Beef rearing

At one time nearly all farms at both side of the valley [Howgill] sold milk. Well now it's just one or two here and there. They've gone more on stock rearing. **Willy Whitwell** b.1914

When milk production declined, beef rearing offered an alternative source of income. This called for a different type of animal and farmers now looked for breeds of cattle that would produce a better carcase. The familiar black and white Friesians, and later Holsteins, could still be seen where milking herds survived, but then cattle of different hues began to appear in the valleys.

When my father first started [in Barbondale] we used to have house cows to supply milk for the house and that was about it, then as time went by he went to France and bought pedigree Charolais… It was a big thing because nobody had ever heard of Charolais. We got the first import of proper Charolais cows from France, then we started breeding bulls and he specialised in breeding Charolais bulls and he become a big name in that area. **Duncan Shuttleworth** b.1955

Stock rearing was less labour intensive than milk production but still required time and effort, especially in winter.

The cows during the winter were kept indoors in a shippon. They would put down a certain amount of bracken, though very often the cows would settle down on the stone settles. But bracken made excellent bedding and certainly all the young

❝ We used to mow bracken to bed calves with. Couldn't afford straw at a shilling a bale ❞

cattle were bedded with bracken which was cut on the side of Winder and brought in carts. **Ingram Cleasby** b.1920

Little calves, you'd go round 'em at night an' if their bedding was dirty you'd t' put some fresh bedding on. We were goin' in at back end [autumn] for brackens down Barbondale wi' t' horse and cart. Brackens were for beddin'. An' that made better muck than rushes, yer know. A lot easier to muck out and everything. **Jack Middleton** b.1921

When we were at Cote Faw [Cowgill] we used to go way up Dent Head to mow rushes to bed calves with. Aye, you couldn't afford to buy any straw and it was only a shilling a bale in those days. **Jim Middleton** b.1913

I used to get that – thou'll never have seen 'em, thou's not old enough – girt slabs o' cake, linseed cake, thou used to have to break 'em up and give 'em it, slide into t' boose [cow stall]. From either Dinsdale's or Edmondson's, whichever they're at. They reckoned four or five in a bag, 'cos they were hessian bags in them days. **Tom Sedgwick** b.1917

Marketing, auction marts and 'luck'

Before auction marts were established stock was often sold direct from the farm.

Richard Turner and one or two people used to come round to buy on the farm what we call spring calvers, calved in spring, come about February, March, and if you bought some, you'd buy maybe two here, three there. Then I can remember walking them to Dent station. Some of them were that weak they couldn't get up that hill, you know [at 1150ft the highest mainline station in England]. It used to be a full day. **Miley Taylor** b.1923

T' new calved cows, we used to drive 'em from Cote Faw [Cowgill] up Station Hill, they went by train to Hawes an' I used to 'elp, an' then come back t' go t' school. I could do it in time t' get back fer nine o'clock. **Jack Middleton** b.1921

From Dent station farmers could take their stock by rail to Hawes or Hellifield. Until

1954 Sedbergh stock, too, could be moved by rail, but Sedbergh also had its own auction mart.

My grandfather made himself into a self-styled valuer and auctioneer, and so he started the business, the auctioneering business. It was in Joss Lane car park then. It was much smaller, it had an assembly room which was just north where the bungalows are now, and the Harper family ran the assembly rooms which we used for selling furniture, as well as small social events I think. That was burnt down during the war, full of furniture… It seemed much roomier than the car park looks because there used to be quite a lot of traffic in and out, and the auction mart had quite a decent size ring and a shippon and sitting places all tiered round it, and the office…

The first one was a very primitive building mainly made of very basic construction, but it served its purpose. And it must have been a great trial to the people who lived round that area, once a week, because there wasn't the hygiene in those days, and I remember going up the town myself on a hot summer Sunday, and the smell was still there from the previous Wednesday. So I think it was probably a good thing when it was moved [to Station Road] where there was a proper water supply and everything provided…

It dealt with all livestock and it was nearly all foot-driven in those days, only something very special came any other way. I mean milking cows, poor things, used to have to walk miles to the auction… At the beginning of the war or just before, the 1930s, a sort of motorised truck seemed to appear, and it had a sort of cabin at the front of this truck and more special animals arrived in that. But there weren't really any cattle wagons until the war – they seemed to originate with the war. And local cows that went to Liverpool to those milk houses had to go to the stations and go on the train. When the auction mart got bigger all the big trucks came past your house on Back Lane. They used to say it was

'The urine ran out of the auction mart and down the street. You could smell Wednesday's market on Sunday!'

a nightmare living on Back Lane when the sheep sales were on, because it used to go on all night I believe, and shake the houses…

A lot of the farmers had ponies and traps and they were related to other farmers on the outskirts of Sedbergh, and so it was a social meeting place for the whole of the area really, because it was the day that the wives went shopping and met their relations and the men all got together and discussed the ins and outs of farming, and sold or bought. It was definitely a little busy market town in those days. **Jean Donald** b. 1921

I remember the old auction mart that was here in Joss Lane car park. I remember the urine coming out of the auction onto the car park, as we went in. I'm not sure it didn't run down the street when there was a lot of cattle about! And sheep, I remember walking sheep to Kendal, even. If we thought there was a better trade at Kendal we'd be traitors and go to Kendal… I remember the first cow I sold, the first new-calved heifer. I brought it to Sedbergh auction and I got to £28, £30 I think it was, £30 it made, and a local farmer bought it from Lincoln's Inn Bridge, and cor blimey, he examined it when he bought it an' he looked over it, he found a lump on the back leg, so bloomin 'eck, to satisfy him I had to give £2 back fer 'luck'! **Myles Jackson** b.1928

Some farmers would go to t' auction and if they thought they were going to 'ave t' pay 'luck' they didn't agree wi' they'd come back home early so they didn't ha' t' pay it! They'd get on t' their bikes, come away afore t' fella got hold on 'em, y' see! **Bessie Mason** b.1911

Bessie Mason moved from Dent to Selside where her family hosted cattle sales. The farm was on a route drovers had used for centuries. By the time Bessie was growing up, after the First World War, the drovers had become drivers, trundling over tarmac instead of following the green tracks.

They used to go and buy cows up in Scotland, at Lanark, and they used to come down in wagons and they 'ad to hunger 'em because there was a big risk when there was this change [to richer grass]. They'd summer 'em, and then they had a sale in September and t' sale used to be 'ere [Selside]. Grannie and them, they baked and everybody got a feed. They 'ad a keg of whisky and special customers got a drink, an' t' other customers 'ad a meal in t' other room. **Bessie Mason** b.1911

Slaughtering

We used to have a cattle dealer called Matt Dinsdale, he farmed at Brigflatts and he used to buy cattle. Well the Irish boats used to come into Heysham full of Irish cattle and also from Scotland with the Aberdeen Angus, Galloway and the long-horned Scotch cattle, into Penrith and Carlisle. Matt, 'e used to go up on the train probably once a month or something in that region and he would buy sufficient cattle to service Sedbergh and district with store or fat cattle, and his son Jim used to go round us lads at the school because they used to come into Sedbergh station into the lairage [holding pens] and they used to let them off out of the lairage, come up Station Road, and we used to turn these cattle at various road ends till they got back to Brigflatts. And the first time I saw Scotch cattle with horns about two yards wide was a cow coming up the station road and meeting us, and we'd to turn the thing down towards Kirkby Lonsdale with these cows!

> *My father would kill the cattle with a poleaxe. No restrictions then*

Matt serviced most of the butchers in the town. We had three butchers in Sedbergh, there was Capstick's, there was Teddy Lane and there was Sanderson, and also we had a number of hawker butchers. There was about five hawker butchers and these lads used to kill these cattle, there was no restrictions then. Most of them had humane killers but a lot of them were just stunned and stuck. And of course they would kill a cow, these butchers, and they would hawk it round the district till they got shot of what they had butchered. There was Bill Woof, there was Jim Mattison, there was Burton from Dent and there was Dan Fleming, and he had a butching shop at Low Oaks at Marthwaite, and they used to hawk around the town and round the district with horse and cart. **Leslie Robinson** b.1930

My father used to kill the cattle with a poleaxe, so e's told me. They 'adn't captive bolt pistols in them days, they used to have a long pole with a weighted spike on the end, y'know, an' they used to get the animal and tie it's 'ead down t' ground with a ring through, into the ground. There's still a ring at Udales [former butcher's shop in Sedbergh] in the ground now. So they 'ad its 'ead right on t' ground and then whoever did it was well practised an' it was a matter of getting this spike right through its forehead first time – they used to have to be a good aim – an' then cutting its throat, so that's how they used to kill 'em. **Garth Steadman** b.1945

If you got livestock you get dead stock. **Reg Charnley** b.1942

CHAPTER 5

Sheep

Heafs – Breeds –
Lambing – Washing, castrating, salving –
Gathering, clipping, dipping – Sales – Yan, tan, tethera –
One man and his dog – Subsidies

*S*heep rearing has always been a mainstay of farming in the dales. It made for a busy life: breeding, lambing, washing, castrating, clipping, salving, not to mention training the dogs that gathered them in from the hills.

On unfenced fells the flocks stay together, each on their own patch, or heaf. Each flock becomes accustomed to its particular heaf through long association. When a farm is sold or rented the heafed sheep remain on the land with the new owner or tenant so that the flock's knowledge of 'their' patch is continued.

Heafs

We have meeting dates for gathering and July clipping time where you take all your stray sheep on to one point and pick them up, and the same applies at tupping time, lambing time probably as well, but the date that sticks to mind is July, first week in July for clipping and there's a date end of October for tupping, them's the two main dates really. Brant Fell Committee sees to it all with a secretary and treasurer etc. Most people put a tag in the ear and there's usually some sort of formal horn-burn in the horn and it would be foolish to change that because nobody's going know whose they are. **Duncan Shuttleworth** b.1955

Every year they had a meeting at Ribblehead for t' gate 'olders. There was eight of 'em. **Bessie Mason** b.1911

You put the lambs out with their mums and they go up there and they get to know their own heaf, and you bring them in and you winter the females and then they go back to the ground they were brought up on. **Duncan Shuttleworth** b.1955

Breeds

When we came to Fell House [Barbondale] they were Dalesbred… They're a speckled face, smaller conformation than a Swaledale, good milking sheep,

"Swaddells at first were nobbut rubbish. Their fleeces had fuzzy edges"

sort of like a dark faced Scot but not so woolly. They were bred to produce a Masham lamb, which were a Teesdale cross or a Wensleydale cross… But we had a terrible problem with Dalesbreds because they had an infection called scrapie, and we weren't used to them and we didn't know the breeding of them. So my father went back to his roots and bought Swaledales, and he got them to the stage where they were pedigree Swaledales… The Swaledale Association is a very big association. We've got the St John's Chapel on the east side, you've got Kirkby Stephen ones more central, and we've got the Hawes ones. They've all got their speciality breeding. **Duncan Shuttleworth** b.1955

We had Swaddells [Swaledales], we've never had nothing else [at Spice Gill, Cowgill]. I had just over fifty and 'appen sixteen gimmer hogs [young female sheep], 'an I knew 'em all by name when I was a lad. [At first] they were nobbut rubbish, a lot of them. Their fleeces had fuzzy edges and they were all sorts of a mixture, now they are more like true to the strain. **Tom Sedgwick** b.1917

I also took an interest in the Rough Fells and I've showed about every show there is to show and I've judged every show that there is to be judged in the Rough side of it. We had a small flock of Roughs – about sixty. I took an interest in them and I took them on to a higher standard. **Duncan Shuttleworth** b.1955

Lambing

About the middle of April [was lambing time] for these high fell farms. And this was soon enough because there was little or no grass for the ewes to feed on, so their milk supply would be threatened. If they started lambing earlier there just wouldn't have been the herbage. Now with bringing sheep into sheep sheds means that they can lamb much earlier, but they can't speed up the growth of the grass. **Ingram Cleasby** b.1920

In lambing time you helped in various ways, to feed bottling lambs or bringing them in, going to see if everything was well. It took priority over everything else. **Betty Harper** b.1920

You 'look the sheep' [inspect them] in one lot and move the lambs to so-and-so,

‟I used to castrate them with a metal clamp thing„

'look the sheep' in another lot, and you had to look them four or five times during the day, and dawn and dusk, and I remember [as a Land Girl in the Second World War] our headman saying 'Start early but make sure of good time in the evening because if you have a difficult case and you are stuck with it, well, it's going to get dark before you get round.' And of course I was working with these men, they were looking other lots, moving lambs and so on in other pastures, but when it got down to the last twenty five they actually handed them over to me and I was in sole charge and, of course, very proud of that. **Helga Frankland** b.1920

Washing, castrating, salving

The next job after lambing was sheep washing. This used to be done two or three weeks before shearing, in June, though today the practice has died out.

I 'ave washed 'em up at Lockin Garth [waterfall in Deepdale], run 'em through. You pushed 'em and they went through – well there's a dub [pool] there. The idea was to get the wool cleaner, but we found it didn't pay, you got it cleaner but you didn't get the weight of wool. **Miley Taylor** b.1923

I used to do that job, castrate 'em. I used t' go t' other parts t' do it. A metal clamp thing, I 'ave it somewhere. It's all greased up. I thought I'll keep that job on, but yer see I'm not allowed to do it now. An' then, I couldn't buy green salve neither. I used t' go through t' chemist, you could buy it at Hawes. **Jack Middleton** b.1921

[Green salve was] to keep out watter really. It like helped weight of wool if it were greasy, thou sees. **Tom Sedgwick** b.1917

Gathering, clipping, dipping

To gather them from a thousand-acre heaf like Wild Boar Fell was extremely arduous on account of the terrain and often needed two teams of dogs along with those of a neighbour. **Ingram Cleasby** b.1920

Aye, they used to go right over the top. You know, where the Calf is [top of the Howgills]. Well they went on the next ridge behind. It was a long job! When we gathered 'em in, we used to reckon if we had a good gather it used to take us about seven hours. Anything went wrong of course it was longer. But usually for clipping days we used to gather 'em in t' night before. If you waited to gather till three o'clock in the morning it was way on into the morning before you got to clipping, so we used to go the night before…

There would 'appen be ten to a dozen come to clip 'ere, and then them people would go to another place, and another place, and you went round. I know I liked the job, I used to get the job at, reckoning up, thirteen or fourteen different places. And then those people came to us. Like a boon day. Oh, you had 'em to feed. And some of the places, they had a bit of a get-together at night. People used to see who could tell the tallest tale or something like that. There was usually a can or two of beer, or bottles in those days. Cans weren't thought of. Sometimes, there was an old chap used to bring his melodeon. **Willie Whitwell** b.1914

This was a great event in the annual work of the farm, because to clip a whole flock by hand was a considerable task, and so it's a feature of these fell farms that families joined together and they'd take turns to go and clip one person's sheep and then another's and they'd be clipping all day. Ideally, there were sheep folds which were surrounded by trees which gave plenty of shade, because it was a very hot business clipping in June, both for the sheep and for the men. A typical fold would have sycamore trees round it, and there they would sit clipping, sitting on a special clipping stool, with the sheep on its back, and would clip away. **Ingram Cleasby** b.1920

But if anybody came to 'elp I 'ad t' clip on t' ground an' give up me stock [clipping stool] to t' man who'd come t' help. **Jack Middleton** b.1921

I used t' look forward t' the clipping time, an' I could darn me stockin's after that 'cause oh, me 'ands were lovely an' greasy! **Jenny Kiddle** b.1918

[The women] would help to roll the fleeces, and then the fleeces would be put in a huge sacking bag which had to be stitched at the top because I remember we had a specially shaped needle, a curved needle. They stitched the top and then somebody used to come round with a lorry to collect them and they probably went to Bradford I would think. It would be quite financially helpful at that time. It isn't now. Sheep's fleeces are worthless. **Betty Harper** b.1920

A fellow from Bradford, Holmes and Rhodes, he would give four pence for a pound [of fleeces], it's selled by weight thou see, but it had been thou couldn't get thre'pence for it and they wouldn't sell it. A van or two wagons came from Bradford, and they took it up to Akrigg's [Ewegales, Cowgill] and they weighed it in that spot there and they paid for it there and then. **Tom Sedgwick** b.1917

The wool cheque was quite important. I got into awful trouble because I happened to mention to a neighbour that the wool cheque was for £500 or whatever. As a kid you got a mighty clout for disclosing these secrets. **Kevin Lancaster** b.1959

❛Dipping was a performance. Black grease and rancid butter❜

I used t' clip them by 'and, an' I learnt t' clip wi' a machine about 1957 an' I've bin clipping wi' a clipping machine ever since. You can soon clip 'em off, but a lot of farmers get contractors in an' they are charging forty five an' fifty pence a sheep. Well, the wool doesn't cover it, an' some farmers are burnin' it! Burnin' the wool rather than sending it in! Well, it's ridiculous! **Reg Charnley** b.1942

In my childhood you relied on the income of your flock and you'd clip the sheep for a profit. Where things have changed now, you clip the sheep as husbandry, you don't get anything. I mean it's a joke what you get for the price of wool. **Duncan Shuttleworth** b.1955

[Dipping] was a performance! They used to buy black grease and they bought rancid butter and t' day o' dipping was, you'd to set boiler on to hot water and you'd a fire going on a stand and you were melting this grease. We had a tub that sheep was lifted in, wooden tub, an' my job was with an alarm clock, an' every sheep had to stop in five minutes and when it was done I had to shout 'Time's up' and then a pan full of this grease was put into t' tub for t' next sheep. **Bessie Mason** b. 1911

Dipping? [We used] Cooper's [Cooper's Border Paste Dip], 'appen, for fly dip and then, 'appen, Young's for mid dip. Aye. Come in a bucket, thou cut it out wi' trowel and then had to soften it wi' hot water. **Tom Sedgwick** b.1917

I've an open dipper but if you're enclosed I'm sure then the fumes 'll get you. I know once, three year ago, I went to Hawes auction, and they were selling the gimmer lambs, which had all been recently dipped, lot o' people enclosed, and I sat there all day. I didn't feel well for a week and I blame that, I do. **Miley Taylor** b.1923

Sales

I used to take my lambs up to Cow Dub [Cowgill], there was a sale there every back end [autumn] which was run by Richard Turner's o' Bentham, and I used to walk the lambs up there [from Deepdale]. There was two grocers in Dent, Dinsdale's and Batty's, and yer got your bill from Batty's once a year once you'd sold yer lambs, when there was a bit o' money in. Lambs were sold then for about half a crown apiece. **Miley Taylor** b. 1923

He [father] sold his sheep at Bentham. They used to walk them. Draughts they called them, draughts, but you couldn't walk them today, too much traffic. **Elizabeth Middleton** b.1915

We used to walk a draught of ewes to Kendal out of Howgill, five flocks together, so that they were easier to manage when there's a large flock because you fill the road and a car can't come just pushing past. I remember one instance when a chap came pushing in and pushing in and the sheep eventually closed in on him. The lad at the back, called Capstick, he says to him 'You seems to be in a hell of a hurry'. He says 'I'm in a desperate hurry'. The lad says 'Aye, tha' should 've set off yesterday'!... Going through Mealbank they went into one of the council houses and they got in the garden, and they went round the house and came back out of the gate again. They just about rotated the garden! We quietly shut the gate and kept on walking! **Robert Taylor** b.1929

"I never did count 'em, I knew 'em all by name"

Just this side of the Dragon [George and Dragon, Dent] they'd sell sheep, and I think Billy Sunter would be the last that selled 'em there or took some. I was seven or eight, 'appen, when they give over selling there. It would be 1920s… Sometimes I bought tups at Kirkby Stephen and sometimes at Hawes and brought 'em back down here [Spice Gill, Cowgill], walked 'em down from the station. 'Appen there was a bit of rope round 'em but I brought 'em down. It was a hard life then. **Tom Sedgwick** b.1917

Yan, tan, tethera…

There are different ways of counting sheep – in fives (five, ten, fifteen, twenty, you know) but you 'ad to be a good 'and at that. I managed to count in threes, usually twos, people would count in twos. There was the old, old method but we never used it, we just heard about it: yan, tan, tethera, hethera, pimp; sethera, lethera, hobbera, dobbera, dick; yan dick, tan dick, tethera dick, methera dick, bumfit; yan bumfit, tan bumfit, tethera bumfit, [methera bumfit], giggot. That's up to twenty! I might have missed one or two out, I'm not sure. That was Celtic wasn't it? **Myles Jackson** b.1928

I never hardly did count 'em, when I was younger I knew 'em all by name and I could tell if they were there or not. **Tom Sedgwick** b.1917

When we 'ad 'em on 'lotments they used t' go round [and count] but I never used t' count 'em because you'd come back an' if you counted 'em there'd be one a missin' an' you would be friggin' about looking fer it, but if yer didn't know it were missin' yer didn't bother t' look fer it! **Jack Middleton** b.1921

"I didn't like subsidies – but I took it!"

One man and his dog

You needed a good sheepdog, which we had. We had one sheepdog which would only work for certain people. But then a lot of them are like that. I remember this old one, my sister Emma could run 'im, I couldn't. And when he got older he got quite bad tempered so you had to be very careful. He used to come into the house, that one. Normally farmers don't like you making a fuss of sheepdogs, making pets of them, because it spoils them for work, but you tend to want to, to make a pet of them if you can. **Betty Harper** b.1920

Well it was dog and stick, so that's all right – stick's broken, dog's lame and that's it! **Myles Jackson** b.1928

Subsidies

Subsidies came in, 'appen in fifties, sixties. It wasn't much they gave you at start, and you 'ad to do things the way they say. It 'asn't done us any good. I didn't like it – but we took it! **Tom Sedgwick** b.1917

Coming from a town, which I did, and I'd only been in the pub [The Sun, Dent] a week or two and you try and get talking with the locals so you can actually bond with them and what have you, and there was a group of old locals talking at the bar about farming and I just happened to say 'Well, how many sheep have you got?'. Well, you'd have thought I'd committed murder! They all turned round and looked at each other, gone purple, because of course I didn't realise, if he'd told me how many sheep he'd got then his mate 'd know how much subsidy he has and that would be war on! So I didn't ever ask again! **Eddie Smith** b.1949

CHAPTER 6

Pigs, poultry and game

The piggeries – The family pig – From pig to pork –
Sharing – Rituals and superstitions – Dual occupation –
Poultry and eggs – Knitting for game

While cattle and sheep were the mainstay, there was more to dales farming than milk and lambing. Nearly every farm had a pig to see the family through the winter, with some making a business of it. And hens would provide eggs for a quick cash return.

The piggeries

Everybody, nearly, kept a pig, even some of the villagers. At Gawthrop I started with one pig and I graduated to about ten or a dozen. I'd no land and I had the piggery at Dent from Frank Dinsdale, until eventually I think I had about two hundred pigs. The piggery near Church Bridge, they were under cover… And then we developed a disease called swine fever and I lost the lot. But I was manufacturing a few concrete blocks and I kept going. **Albert Fothergill** b.1923

There was a piggery at Dent run by a chap called Albert Fothergill. We'd run out o' pigs or we were running short o' pigs for Christmas. We went up Dent and we knocked about six, I think, and we hadn't got a humane killer, so dad had t' claw hammer an' he dropped each one, one blow between the eyes. He dropped 'em, then cut their throats an' that was it, y' know, they were done. Then we'd to boil 'em, we scraped them and brought them 'ome. We were selling 'em next day [in Steadman's butcher's shop, Sedbergh]. Aye such were the days! **Garth Steadman** b.1945

The family pig

> *You were killing a friend really, but it was worth it for the sausages*

We always kept two pigs. I had a Gert and Daisy and I always had 'em named. Oh I didn't like when we 'ad to kill pigs, I always went out of hearing. I fed 'em all an' they all got spoiled, they'd lie down when I went in fer me to rub their tummies an' if anybody else went in they'd have gone for 'em, some of 'em! Oh, that's our life, wasn't it, I loved animals and I made pets of 'em all… Yes, the man killed it at home and then cut it up, you know, hung it up. I didn't mind once I got it hung up, didn't look a bit like a pig at all when they get them opened and hung up, so I kept away till it got done with. **Mary Ellison** b.1909

We lived off our own eggs and milk and bacon, and pig-killing day was a bit of a sad day, you were killing a friend really, but it was worth it for the sausages and black puddings! A chap called Jack Thwaite that lived in Grisedale came, and what a spotlessly clean chap he was in his killing! I'd left school before I was brave enough to catch blood. Washhouse had a big boiler and they couldn't start pig-killing until the water was hot. Then all the neighbours came, a certain woman would make potted meat, another would make sausages, another would make black pudding, and when they killed theirs the circuit went round again, there'd be a riot on if they hadn't a done that… It just seemed to happen, everybody knew what everybody was good at… At every occasion there was a tea party, the home-baked bread and apple pasty that had plenty of sugar in it. **Dick Harrison** b.1934

You were allus t' kill a pig when there was an 'r' in t' month, on account of flies, yer see. October was a wee bit early, November was the more usual month. Your second one would be killed in March an' yer would never go after March on account of flies getting about. Yer'd t' watch that, yer know. **Cissy Middleton** b.1914

If you'd a dead pig in t' 'ouse and a wick wife you were alright for the winter!

We didn't breed any pigs. [Father] used t' buy 'em in the spring, usually at Dent Fair Day, 'e bought two pigs an' bring 'em back. There was a man who used t' come with pigs an' 'e used t' buy 'em off 'im, then fatten 'em an' then kill 'em. An' 'e used t' kill 'em 'imself. If yer didn't kill 'em when there was an 'r' in the month there was bloodwashers [flies] about and they would strike with maggots, yer see. Aye, 'e used t' go around killin' pigs. And Matt Haygarth at Rivelin [Cowgill] 'e used to do it, an' Jack Akrigg did as well. Oh you couldn't do without a pig! They said if you'd a dead pig in t' 'ouse and a wick [lively] wife yer were alright fer winter! **Jack Middleton** b.1921

My mother-in-law, when the time came to kill the pig she went away for the day, she couldn't bear to be at home thinking that the pig she'd carefully fed all this time was being killed! But some people next to where I lived on the hill kept a pig and they used to kill it out in the open, and – bloodthirsty young kids – when we heard this pig squealing because it had been probably stabbed in the throat or something, we used to all dash to see what was happening, although she'd been cut up and bled and all. It's terrible when you think about it. But it was quite an occasion, a pig killing. **Marjorie Middleton** b.1913

It was the smell of blood in the first place that sort of half upset me and then when they slit it down the middle to take all the entrails out it just overcame me, and I just remember hanging over the orchard wall bringing all me breakfast up, and I disappeared indoors for the rest of the day! All the little bits that were cut off were all fried in a big pan of oil, just like pork scratchings but crackling… it was crisp, yes. And when you think about them now they were lovely, but when Mary arrived with this bowl of chitterlings, they used to call them, and said 'Brought you these!' and I got a sniff of those, whoa! I was away again! I was nobbut a kid yet! **Bob Turner** b.1933

From pig to pork

Cissy Middleton recalls in detail, and with relish, how every part of the pig, from head to toe, was used to keep the family fed.

First thing yer did when you were going t' kill a pig, yer set boiler on, yer washing boiler, yer 'ad t' 'ave that full of boiling water by time they were going t' kill a pig. Somebody would be there ready with a bucket an' a stick, p'raps a pint of milk an' a saucer full of salt so that when they killed the pig they would run the blood an' yer would catch it in a bucket an' yer would 'ave t' stir an' stir an' stir, put this milk in an' this salt in to stop it curdling, but sometimes it curdled on you, but if it did then you jus' put it through a sieve and that was fer black puddins…

Then the pig was all scraped wi' this boiling water, an' all hair an' that was all scraped off until they were absolutely clean, an' when all got taken off then they slung it up an' it 'ad t' stay there fer at least twenty-four hours to a day an' a half t' hang, t' drip an' everything, an' get properly set, an' then t' following day they would come an' saw it down the centre an' then it was all laid out, they would 'ave a sheep's stool an' lay out one 'alf an' then they would tek all t' ribs out an' shape it out, an' then they cut the hams an' flitches an' shoulders…

For curing it would be teken down in t' cellar an' turned upside down so that every drop of blood drained from it, yer didn't put its skin on top so any juices ran out, and then you would 'ave so much saltpetre to buy an' we got this rock salt, we used t' buy a big chunk, about a fourteen pound block of ordinary cooking salt. A big, thick block! Well, us young ones we used t' 'ave t' chop it up an' mek it fine an' put it into a dish ready for them an' you rubbed first a little bit, yer turned end up and took marra [marrow] out at bone's end an' filled it up wi' saltpetre. An' then yer turned them an' get skin up that way an' then yer put a little bit o' saltpetre on an' yer rubbed an' rubbed an' rubbed till it got t' what we call 'sweating', it got all moist on top. An' then when that was done yer rubbed in so much ordinary salt. Yer didn't pinch. And yer give flitches about eight to ten days an' then yer took it out, give it a good washing down, brought it up t' sink an' cold water an' got all your salt off, dried it an then rolled it up. Yer med a roll of it an' tied it with string an' then they were 'ung up on 'ooks, we'd 'ooks in t' 'ouse to 'ook an' dry them. Well you'd got moisture comin' so then we 'ad t' get some material an' wrap it round bottom so we didn't get any mess onto t' floor from any drips till it really got dried. But oh, a week or so an' then it was grand! There was nothing like it!

> *Pig foot pie... Take the toenails off, wash and scrub them, season with black pudding and onions*

When yer med yer black puddins yer didn't do it first day… A good butcher would clean all the intestines for yer, if yer wanted them, they were all turned inside out an' washed an' cleaned an' everything… After a day or two yer boiled a big pan full of barley an' yer chopped a lot of the fat up from the pig, what you thought was necessary. It wasn't a good idea t' pinch it, the more fat yer put in, lighter yer black puddins were, an' then yer seasoned them. Sometimes we got chopping an onion up and putting it in an' you put sage an' thyme an' marjoram in fer seasoning. Oh they were good were black puddins! You'd smell 'em fer far enough! Mother used t' put 'em in skins but I never did. We just baked them in a bread tin an' then cut it in slices, but I can remember me mum 'avin' them hung up on 'ooks in t' living rooms an' you would jus' go and get a black puddin when yer wanted one!

[For potted meat and sausages] head was cut off first, we used t' mek it into brawn an' potted meat. We used t' buy about a couple of pounds of beef t' put into that t' mek it a lot better… There were some lovely frying bits that would be cut out an' then you could mek sausages with that. I had a thing t' put on me machine that jus' med 'em flow out an' fill yer sausages…

Yer got all this lines of fat out of t' pig… But fat out of t' ribs, that were solid fat so yer cut that up as fine as yer could, an' then that was put into a pan an' rendered down, put through a colander and into a great big stone pot an' that was yer lard fer winter. And in wartime a lot of people would come when they were short of fat, 'Yer don't 'ave such a thing as a pot of fat, do you?' 'cos they were short of lard. An' we'd 'ave given many a body a pot of lard or bacon fat t' help them out with rations.

An' then of course yer 'ad pig foot pie. I dunno whether anybody knows about pig foot pie? They killed the pig an' butcher would take all the toenails off. They were all washed an' scrubbed an' perfectly clean. An' then yer boiled them, seasoned them, but yer always put a bit of black pudding in t' that, an' there would be onions in, an' then yer put a crust on top, an' they were good, was a pig foot pie. But they were too rich fer some people! I know one chap med 'imself poorly with 'em but 'e would 'ave jus' eaten them as they were, boiled. It wasn't really a meaty dish, there was little bits of meat yer got in, but very little. It was more like a fatty jelly, an' they were good! **Cissy Middleton** b.1914

Yer used everything but the squeak of the pig when yer butchered it. **Elizabeth Middleton** b.1915

Sharing

We used to help one another with pig killing, nearly every farm kept a pig in those days so you 'ad a pig killing day. Well of course we'd no fridges and so all the offal part of the pigs, the brawn, the black puddings, spare rib, we'd share these out with our neighbours and then when they had a pig killing day they shared it with us, and so it went on through the valley. **Kenneth Cragg** b.1936

Reg Charnley walling in Cowgill. 'It's a skill an' it's either in yer or it's not in yer to do it. Dent stone is the finest walling stone there is' [A]

Miley Taylor at Butterpots, Deepdale. 'Catch the horse, milk the cattle, cut the hay... It was slavery, but I loved it! [B]

Betty Hartley in her kitchen at Cage, Dentdale. 'People still talk about my vanilla slices now!' [C]

Cissy Middleton, Gawthrop: 'Oh, they were good, my black puddings! You'd smell them from far enough!' [D]

George and Mary Ellison of Greenwell, Dent. 'We met at a chapel harvest sale up at Cowgill. Went out for five years... Aye, she was worth waiting for' [E]

Five year old Bob Ellison, son of George and Mary, in charge of his grandfather's home-made cart, sitting on a hamper of poultry. [E]

Elizabeth 'Tizza' Middleton, Deepdale Head: 'I had one of the thrills of my life when I washed with an electric washer. Life changed altogether!' [C]

Teenage Marjorie Middleton. 'Mother made jams – I can remember stirring and stirring!' [B]

Mary Cowperthwaite, Garsdale Hall: 'You had to cross the road to our toilet – an earth closet' [F]

Sedbergh auction mart, Joss Lane, on the site of the present car park [B]

Farmers at the new mart on Station Road, now Spar and the Medical Centre [C]

Loading hay...

...and a pause for 'bait' ('bite-on') time. 'Ten o' clocks we used to call it' [B]

A sheep gather in the Howgills. 'It was a long job. For clipping days we used to gather them in the night before' [B]

Fettling up a hay sled in the Howgills [B]

Sharpening scythes in School Field, Dent in 1891. 'They used to tar it and sprinkle sand on. Yer put a finer sharp edge on' [B]

'Dent rakes had twelve teeth, but the Cowgill ones had fourteen or sixteen because they were more efficient on the short herby grass on the higher hillsides' [A]

Foot cocks at Cowgill, and Lea Yeat Quaker Meeting House where, in the silent meeting, 'nivver nowt 'appened' [B]

Haytime at Hobsons, Cowgill. 'I liked haymaking with the horse, but I liked it better when we got a tractor and I could roll around the field' [A]

Charlie Oversby and friends sheep washing at the Dub, Cowgill. 'You pushed them and they went through' [B]

Shearing in the Howgills. 'I could darn me stockings after clipping, 'cause oh, me hands were lovely and greasy' [B]

A Gloucester Old Spot and her piglets under vet's inspection [C]

Ennis Bentham mucking out at Docklesyke, Deepdale [C]

A boon day at Howgill. 'All the social life in the dale was based on chapels or the church' [B]

An annual church or chapel outing to Morecambe in Burrow's adapted 'Hackney carriage'. 'The highlight of the year! Like going to the moon!' [B]

Children crossing the Lune on their way to Lowgill school. 'There was a box on wires and a rope pulley. If I'd dropped in that would have been it!' [B]

'Sticking': collecting firewood on horse-drawn sled in Howgill. 'Right from being small, we'd to go and fetch a few sticks in' [B]

Dent Band of Hope. 'They would talk about not taking strong drink. I signed the pledge at about nine years old, and I've kept it' [B]

'National Depository': Dent's first public convenience [B]

Boys collecting water at Joss Lane, Sedbergh [B]

DENT SPORTS and RACES

Saturday, June 3rd, 1961

Commencing at 2-30 p.m. prompt.

President:
A. V. HOGARTH, Esq.

COMMITTEE:

E. Akrigg, J. Akrigg, sen., J. Allen, W. Bayne, J. Bentham, N. Brooksbank, A Booth, R. R. Burrow, J. Capstick, J. E. Cookson, W. E. Ellison, M. Hartley, D. Hartley, J. Hartley, J. Mattinson, J. Middleton, J. Murdoch, M. Raw, D. Staveley, D. Parkinson, R. Parrington, J. Thompson.

Secretary and Treasurer:
K. McCLURG

PROGRAMME — 1/-

Westmorland Gazette Ltd., Printers, Kendal

Jack Thompson driving the herd home at Hill Top, Deepdale [B]

I went out one morning to the pigsty when the pig was nearly ready for killing. It was dead. That was a catastrophe. I came in to tell the missus and I said 'Well, we'll have to bury it'. I said 'I can't drag the bloody thing out myself', so she came and we dragged it down just below the house and I dug a hole, put it in, and that night me neighbour came across, and he was saying 'How's pig doing'? and the little girl just said 'Pig dead'. I never will forget that. You see, the pig, you relied on it for your food you know. The hams and the bacon, and specially the fat for baking with, making bannocks. It was a catastrophe. I know me neighbour lent me – no, he *gave* me – half a pig. That was a lot. That was a hell of a lot, you know, then! **Miley Taylor** b.1923

Yer shared out with a lot of people. Anybody else that 'ad a pig, you would give them a piece. We shared a lot, a bit 'ere an' a bit there, so when they killed a pig they brought you a bit back. You weren't wasting anything. An' instead of getting tired of it you 'ad a bit o' rest. You got a taste of theirs an' it was like something new again! **Cissy Middleton** b.1914

It was the custom to give the spare rib to neighbours, and when they killed a pig they brought you spare ribs, so you had fresh pork. But things like hams and thighs were cured and just hung up in the kitchen and sliced up. **Marjorie Middleton** b.1913

Rituals and superstitions

"I turned our swimming pool into a pig sty"

After they'd hung t' pig up, before they opened it, me mother used to ha' to bring round a bowl of whisky and 'ot water, was like a punch bowl, an' this basin would come and we'd all to sup at it, and me an' Jim didn't like it and me grandfather med us sup it. They 'ad the idea it 'elped it to cure, 'cos every pig, you see, didn't cure if they didn't do it. Just a fad. Of course, the butcher an' them as was 'elping 'ad it! **Bessie Mason** b.1911

I remember there used to be funny customs. For example, they would never let a woman who had her periods near the curing of a pig. She wasn't allowed to touch the killing. This is what I heard in Cheshire, that it would affect the curing. **Isobel Stacey** b.1932

Dual occupation

Although pig-rearing was mostly for domestic consumption, some people saw it as a commercial opportunity. It required little land, and for those with enough energy and determination it could be run as a second business alongside their main occupation.

For two or three years I was growing mushrooms in order to make ends meet and to pay my mortgage, but I wasn't able to work them properly for a third year so I had to go over to pigs and that's where my connection with Farfield Mill started again. In 1949 I bought Beamsmoor which was opposite the mill gate. I built a swimming bath for the kids which I had to turn into a pig sty. I had about fifty pigs in this at a time, so I had to go to Farfield Mill which had been turned into a cheese factory. Early fifties, 1952, 1953. I used to get a hundred gallons of whey every day and I made myself a wheelbarrow with thick tyres and I had three kits of whey – that was thirty-six gallons at a time – and you could push it over there and push it back. And eventually, after some years, I would get a little conveyor, motor conveyor, which would take a hundred gallons at a time, so life eased a little bit. I was teaching at the time. I was very busy. I used to keep the pigs for bacon, and off they went. I sent them to Cavaghan and Gray at Carlisle. **Dick Kevan** b.1914

Poultry and eggs

Tony Edmondson used to come to a room which is now a holiday cottage, just round the corner from the school [in Dent], and farmers' wives used to bring down butter and eggs, and that was their house-keeping money really. **Marjorie Middleton** b.1913

I know we 'ad a lot of 'ens, we always kept a lot of 'ens, a few 'undred, and so had a lot of boxes of eggs a week and they all went to Appleby and another lot for 'atching to Lumbs, Hebden Bridge. It always took me an hour or two at night to clean all the 'ens, I'll tell you! White leghorns and Rhode Island Red, and some were crossed and some were pure. **Mary Ellison** b.1909

I thought, well, we want something that'll bring some cash in quite easily, quite early, so I got five 'undred [hens] that year. I was poultry woman, done it at 'ome, with incubators an' I knew 'ow t' go about things. An' it was a boon, was that, because when yer got into a hatchery you got paid a lot better for your eggs, an' we survived! **Cissy Middleton** b.1914

❛Eggs were making more than sheep and cattle❜ They stopped us selling milk and that was a big blow but at that time poultry had become a big thing so we went into keeping quite a lot of poultry and hatching eggs, and Bertie Gornall from Cowgill used to come and take them every Saturday morning, and he took 'em to a firm called Harlings at Sandside, and we built up until we'd nearly a thousand hens, and that became as good an income as what the milk had been. All free range, in cabins of various sizes and an old out-barn. And then the surplus eggs which weren't fit for hatching, because they all had to be weighed and a certain size, anything over that went to Express Dairies from Appleby. So we 'ad two lots of eggs going every week and that was a good business. **Kenneth Cragg** b. 1936

We'd about five 'undred [hens]. We were selling the eggs fer 'atching. The 'en was a main crop, wasn't it? They were t' best cashing things, eggs. We were getting about sixpence a dozen or more. They were making more than sheep and cattle… But that didn't last for ever, it packed in. **Jim Middleton** b.1913

I worked for an egg-packing station at Birks Mill [Sedbergh]. There was a war on and I was in the army when it was moved from Garsdale Head. They had their own little petrol engine and their own electrics and the egg-grading machine worked off it, and we thought we were upmarket, electric light! It was more like a warehouse than anything, and the railway houses [at Garsdale] only had candles and lamps. The eggs came from the farms round about but we went into Leeds every Friday morning and there wasn't the quantity of things like now, we used to go down Wensleydale on the Great North Road, you could have gone down there blindfold really, and we'd go round the shops as it got better and better, supply them with eggs. They were rationed, you got one egg each for a week. Well, one egg wasn't much if you ate it boiled, was it? When things got better we had that many eggs we'd go Friday with a truckload and again on Saturday with another… It was run under the Ministry of Food, we were never stuck with them at all, and controlled prices were on. I finished in 1956 and went as a postman till I retired [in1991]. **Dennis Abbott** b.1926

We grew turkeys. We used to have a terrific dressing at Christmas, getting up in the morning early, dressing these birds. When [daughter] Rosalie was born, she was born on New Year's Day, and [husband] Douglas says, 'You'll get these dressed afore you go to hospital, won't you?'. We used to rear about thirty or forty. Oh we had some terrible plucking do's, the amount of time spent on them! You see, we did all sorts to raise money! But I liked plucking turkeys. They used to look good when they were done. We used to take a lot over Settle way. They used to give them as presents to the staff so they had to look nice. **Betty Hartley** b.1913

> *Father knitted a mile of netting to net grouse*

Knitting for game

You got a licence to put nets up and caught grouse you see, they were always worth a lot, we sold 'em to London. We had to pack 'em in a box and get 'em to station and send 'em on train to London and they were what helped us out. There'd only be a box with four or five grouse in and maybe a pigeon or two, they didn't want partridge or things like that, there were greyhens and partridge and they had half brown meat and half white so they didn't want them so we ate them, and they were good! **Mary Ellison** b.1909

Things were pretty tight at the end of the war and we did a lot of shooting, snaring, netting, we used to net grouse and netting was legal at that time. I used to have a mile of nets set up on the fells for the grouse an' father, he knit all these himself. Balls of string he used to get, he was very, very quick. These grouse nets are four foot six deep, he could knit a yard forward every hour, used to sit for hours at night with just the old paraffin lamp and he'd sit making nets. The needles that they wrapped the string on, they're big, broad knitting needles and the string, with a spike in the middle and the string wraps round…

A grouse net is a two inch mesh net, twenty foot long and four foot six deep.

You had poles like broom handles ten foot high, they had a little spring clip on the top and half way down. You put the poles one foot into the ground, so that left you with nine foot out. The nets were strung across the top so that the sheep could walk underneath. Grouse usually fly at around seven foot following the contours, at least we knew the places where they came through at about that height, and they used to set these poles and nets, and each net as a rule caught one grouse. When it hit the net, the whole net collapsed and the grouse rolled up in it. Sometimes you'd be lucky and get two but very rare, usually one and we would set long lines of nets out on our own land. We had land up on Rise Hill, we had land in Barbondale which he had rented and we'd land on the Cragg which was rented and he used to have his nets set on these...

We checked them every day because they were still alive. You would often put them up in a morning and you would go and take them up again at night, or sometimes we would leave them up but you'd go next morning. The grouse that we caught were all packed in boxes and sent to London on the railway from Dent station or by post. You could send by post up to fifteen pound weight and I've seen us cutting pieces of cardboard off it to try and get it down to fifteen pound.
Kenneth Cragg b.1936

They used to set nets to catch grouse in t' season. It was good, but it was all bike, you 'ad to get bloody push-bike out, and after nine o' clock on a pushbike Longstone Fell was a hundred yards higher up! **Dick Harrison** b.1934

CHAPTER 7

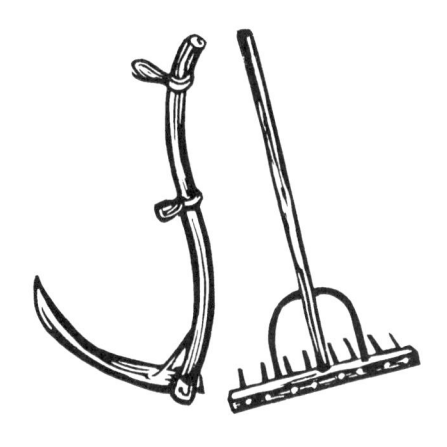

Haytime

A serious business – Scythes – Rakes and sledges –
Mowing, scaling, leading – And then there were tractors –
Plats, pikes, cocks and kemmins – Dialect terms –
Stacking the moo – When the sun wouldn't shine –
Haytime refreshments – Helping the neighbours

When to cut the grass for hay was perhaps the most important decision of the farming year, not helped by the uncertain dales weather. A good hay crop meant there would be feed for the cattle in their winter stalls and extra nutrition for the sheep when grass was no longer growing. A poor crop, or none, spelt disaster. 'Haytiming' before modern machinery was highly labour-intensive and it was a case of everyone lending a hand.

A serious business

If it was an early haytime our school holidays were early. If it was a late season our holidays were late. They used to rope us in. Yes, they used to fix the holidays, did the school managers, 'cos they were all farmers! **Willie Whitwell** b.1914

A lot of farmers in those days used to have to hire an Irishman for the month. As all the work was to do by hand you needed more people and thousands of men used to come over from Ireland for a month for the haymaking season here. Most of the Irishmen were Catholics and they used to have suits to go to church in, different to what they wore when they were haymaking. And if the weather was bad farmers used to get them to whitewash the shippons out, clean out the buildings, till the weather was suitable to make the hay. **Betty Hartley** b.1913

Any visitor to the farm during haytime who did not want to help with the hay we thought very little of indeed. Haytime was an extremely serious business. **Helga Frankland** b.1920

Scythes

Me dad used t' tell me they didn't have a mowing machine. They did all the land with the scythe. **Eva Middleton** b.1923

The only thing he [an employer] looked for was if you could milk and mow with a scythe. If you couldn't mow with a scythe you were no good to him. **Fred Taylor** b.1927

We'd cut a lot with scythes, we all could use scythes, round the edges of the fields, for you didn't leave anything in haytime, you went and cut it off, what they called piking. **Kenneth Cragg** b.1936

Oh there were some good scythe mowers at Cowgill. If yer were a good scythe mower yer could ask fer more money, an' yer got it! Yer used t' get this sand fer sharpening yer strittle [blade], strittle would need sharpening, yer used to get sand off Whernside. They used to tar it an' then sprinkle sand on. Yer put a finer sharp edge on. **Jack Middleton** b.1921

In those days they mew everything out, every corner with the scythe. It was a kind of a sickle wasn't it? There was attachments on the scythe handle to carry it with, it was part of the set-up. **Elizabeth Middleton** b.1915

Cutting the hay would have been with six foot scythes, and I've heard my father say that the men would go into the meadow at four o'clock in the morning with these huge scythes and work all day, mowing the hay. A lot of work! **Ingram Cleasby** b.1920

'They made me a rake when I was three, so I went out and turned ends'

If the weather was fine you'd get up in a morning, soon as was light, you'd take the scythe, and go down the side of the field, both sides, 'cos the horse couldn't pull it all. Then you would come back and catch the horse, and cut some, and then you would milk the cattle. It was slavery. You wouldn't do it now! But I used to like cutting with a scythe, used to love it. **Miley Taylor** b.1923

Rakes and sledges

The work was done by hand rakes, wooden-toothed hand rakes, and forks, either shortish ones for breaking out hay, scattering it in other words, if it were in cocks, or long ones for forking up on to a high load. They really were quite long, with two prongs. But they were beautiful, elegant, curved heads. The shafts of course were wooden. **Helga Frankland** b.1920

They were very famous were Dent rakes, made by Billy Middleton, was it, and Ronnie Haygarth. In the joiner's shop in Dent, where Albert Fothergill's house is today, behind Rhumes where Marjorie Middleton lived, there was a big wood yard there, they could cut all their own trees, saw them up and then make the Dent rakes, and they were well known all over. **Kenneth Cragg** b.1936

Willie Middleton o' joiners at Dent were famous fer rake makin' an' men 'ad their big rakes, but we little ones, we only wanted one height of our selves, which wasn't so big an' not so many teeth in. They made me a rake when I was three and so I went out and turned ends and they said I could take a little bit and turn it weel ower, and I did. **Cissy Middleton** b.1914

Dent hay rakes, going back to the 1800s, really were the Rolls-Royces of rakes, made by Dent joiners and sold all over northern England. They were made of pine, ash, oak and sometimes elm. The shaft was originally pitch pine, later superseded by Columbian pine which was lighter and smoother, so fewer blisters! The head was made from young straight-grained ash grown in the dale, and the teeth were made from local seasoned oak. The Dent rake had twelve teeth, but the ones made at Cowgill had fourteen or sometimes sixteen because they were more efficient on the short herby grass on the higher hillsides. It was said that in the old days you got paid a farthing for every hundred teeth you made...

Cowgill rakes were made by Richard Bayne until the end of the First World War, then by his son in law, my grandad Bobby Middleton. Dent rakes were made by Mr Oversby at Cage farm, Willie Middleton and Harry Burrow, and finally by Ronnie Haygarth, all at the joiners' wood yard in the Laning. I've handled lots of rakes in my time but Ronnie Haygarth's were the best – even better than my grandad's! **Bob Ellison** b.1935

I would sit meking rake teeth – you'd 'em all to hammer through, and I could put 'em in. You sharpened them, and you had the boules that you put in a head and through the handle, you had those to make and steam. You used to set boiler on and put them in there till you could bend 'em. You were lucky if they didn't split, they were awful. They'd just let you get 'em bent and then split up! There was a lot to a rake and we only got two and eleven for 'em, didn't we? They were only

"Me mum and dad used to get up at 3 or 4 in the morning to start mowing before the heat of the day"

two and six and two and eleven pence, and all that hours and hours of work that went into 'em… You bought [the shafts] as a square piece of wood and then you had to plane till they got round. That nearly had me beat, had that. It was a thin rake, we had to get the heads, stuff you med heads of, and teeth, you had to get 'em years before and saw 'em up. We sew [sawed] them up at t' workshop and dry 'em. Put 'em away and forgot about 'em till they got well dried up, very hard. **Mary Ellison** b.1909

[Willie Middleton in Dent] used to make all the sledges, 'cos we didn't use carts for hay, we all used sledges and they made all our sledges. We had smaller ones for pulling with the Galloways, some farmers 'ad bigger horses an' bigger sledges, but that's what we 'ad. **Kenneth Cragg** b.1936

Our ground was steep and awkward so you had to know what you were doing. And that's why we used sledges instead of carts because a cart would have turned over in no time but with sledges you could afford to go on steeper ground. **Helga Frankland** b.1920

Mowing, scaling, leading

We just had one horse, Tommy he was called. It was to mow with machine and in those days you had to start off with a scythe so horse could get through the gate. Me mum and dad used to get up at three or four in the morning to start mowing before the heat of the day. Then they'd have to come out, get horse unhitched, bring cows in to milk and breakfast, so it was a hard life. **Alan Mattinson** b.1934

We used to keep Gallowers [Galloways], not always the black ones but we had a piebald Gallower type horse up to fourteen hands, and for mowing the grass me father used to buy a single horse machine but then put a limber pole on it an' use two Gallowers to pull it, an' it made it so much easier. We always cut the grass with one of those. **Kenneth Cragg** b.1936

[Father] 'ad his mowing machine for two horses. Well, one was a big horse and the other was like a pony thing, Captain and Blossom. **Elizabeth Middleton** b.1915

You first mow a field clockwise from the outside to the middle and the horses walking on the left of the mown hay. The mown hay is then gathered up by the helpers coming after the machine, as it is very important never to tread on any hay. **Helga Frankland** b.1920

> *Bad tempered men med bad tempered horses*

Hay was led [to the barn] by 'orses, you'd 'ave two 'orses on t' bigger farm, an' yer usually rode on t' 'orseback an' you'd t' mind when you went through a gapstead [gateway] you didn't catch it, an' often you walked, like when you'd a full load, but you always rode back an' you 'ad to watch out if a 'orse wanted t' jus' have a nibble while you were on t' 'orseback. I've seen many a time yer go 'ead o'er 'eels, over the 'orse's 'ead! It would just stand still, it wouldn't bother you, it jus' got used t' what it 'ad t' do! **Cissy Middleton** b.1914

They were quite interesting characters were those two horses we had! Molly was the big one and she was a bit unpredictable, you had to be very careful with her, she wasn't very good tempered. The older one was very placid, you could do anything with her! I remember once we were leading hay and my little brother was sitting on the horse – he was only two, I think, or maybe three – in between the rows and Fanny put her head down like that and he fell over down the horse right onto the ground in front of her and she didn't turn a hair! They were fell ponies, I think you'd call them Fell Galloways. **Betty Harper** b.1920

Bad tempered men med bad tempered horses they said, an' I think they did. Took a lot o' training, didn't they? They used to take 'em up to t' station to hear trains set off an' shunt an' that, so they weren't startled. An' once they say a horse 'as bolted it'll bolt again – an' that's what me brother Jack used to say about marriages, he said once a wife bolted she'd bolt again! **Bessie Mason** b.1911

There would be somebody leading the horse or riding it, very often a haytime boy, a boy of perhaps ten or eleven or twelve, that sort of age, or anybody competent to lead the horse. On the fells it was always called 'leading hay', whether it was carted or on a sled. The idea being, you were always leading the horse even if you were driving it on long reins or riding on its back, you were still 'leading hay'! **Helga Frankland** b.1920

My grandfather went to the Great Exhibition of 1851 and brought back with him the first mowing machine which was known in Westmorland, or so I'm told. That must have made a great difference. They're horse drawn, usually with two horses, though on the small farms they were often just a single horse. And they had a cutting, a reciprocating cutting bar, which was very efficient, but of course it was liable to be damaged by the stones, much more so than the present rotary mowers. **Ingram Cleasby** b.1920

'I remember me dad gettin' t' first scaler in Dent'

My dad used to get up early on a fine summer's morning and get his horse harnessed and put into the mowing machine and then he used to go to mow. Somebody had to be there to rake off as he cut it, so when he came round again he knew where to go, and that was a horrible job because there was always midges, it was terrible early in the morning. After that when it got dried a bit we had to strow it all out and then next we had to turn it. Then if it had kept fair for two or three days we had to make it into big windrows [the rows of hay created by rake or mower], then we used to take a horse and sledge and put the hay onto the sledge, tie it with a rope and take it to the barn. Then they had to fork it into the barn and someone had to be inside the barn to scatter it round and tread it down **Mary Cowperthwaite** b.1924

You'd t' scale it by hand an' you'd ter turn it by hand, an' yer'd t' do everything by hand! It took a long time if you'd three acres, which was quite a good bit o' ground, an' unless you'd a few o' you t' do it, you didn't make a mark!… I remember me dad gettin' t' first scaler [spreader], an' that would probably be 1930s, an' it was a big machine – well I wouldn't say out t' ordinary big, but it 'ad a big sort of hood, an' it brought this hay out an' it give it a good scalin', we thought that were super! An' I think that were about t' first one that ever came into Dent. **Cissy Middleton** b.1914

Machinery began to come in, I suppose the first machine that was designed was a strewer, or scaler, and that had an axle, two wheels, shafts, and on this axle there were about four combs, slightly flexible big combs. These prongs were about nine inches apart maybe and as the wheels turned the combs went round and that scattered the hay, up to a point. It wasn't as good as hand-working and it was very hard work for the horses, it was heavy work. And then the other thing that was designed was a side delivery, which was really quite a dangerous implement because it had its two wheels and it had a kind of combs set vertically which moved to and fro, parallel with the axle, so that the hay was cast out on either side and made into windrows automatically, but it only had one wheel in front and so the shafts came round in a curve. They were metal and were attached to part of the framework with this front wheel, and that was not at all stable! On a hillside this wretched thing could very easily turn over. I don't think it ever had a seat on it. Mowing machines had seats. Then once you've led the hay you went over the field with a jinny rake which had a straight shaft in front dividing into two wooden bars going out in a triangular shape and attached to a wooden bar carrying steel prongs, and you just pulled this thing along and the hay gathered up in this sort of curvature of the steel prongs bit and you made a succession of rows across the field. When it got full then you just backed it off a little bit and left the hay there and then when you came round again you left it alongside so that when people went to collect that with the sledge they didn't have to dot all over the field, they just went along these two or three rows. But that was always done, there was nothing left on the ground…

Then we got horse rakes and these were quite fun because you always used a nice, active, lively sort of horse to do the job and it could go along at a fair speed, walking of course, but at a good brisk pace because it wasn't heavy work. The principle was much the same. You did have a seat, you could ride on it and you had a foot lever which raised the combs, so to speak, which was shaped not unlike a jinny rake, but much bigger, and when you put your foot down, it lifted that whole lot and the hay simply fell out and, again, you left it in rows. So those were the two ways of finishing off the field – assuming the weather was fine! **Helga Frankland** b.1920

If we were leadin' hay from Barth Bridge [Dent] we 'ad t' use a cart but any fields nearer then yer just went with sled. Sometimes they used a sweep an' swept it in, somebody guided a big flat thing with big spikes on an' they'd two 'andles an' they jus' went up a row an' got as much as they could an' then took it off an' then away up t' barn, that saved a lot o' loadin' up! But as a rule it were sledded if it were near a barn an' tied up with string – an' sometimes yer'd an accident, if they didn't tie it up properly it would tipple over onto yer…

I remember next thing we got machinery where it got the hay into a box thing an' it just blew it out in a big long stream, which lighten'd yer hay up an' we thought that was fine an' good, then yer got a side rake where it put it all into rows for yer…

Somebody told us they'd got a baler at Low Hall an' that was summat out t' ordinary! We'd a big field, it was a seven acre field, an' we'd a great lot o' hay ready t' come, an' I remember me 'usband makin' enquires, would it be possible by chance fer 'em t' come an' bale us hay, an' they did, an' that set it goin' fer balers comin' in t' Dent. I think they were first t' get a baler at Low Hall an' we thought that was marvellous! I would say 1960s probably, I can't remember which year. **Cissy Middleton** b.1914

> *We got a little grey Fergie – well that was like goin' to heaven!*

Oh aye, it changed a lot, it was just a horse and sled job when I was a lad. When I took o'er father said 'Doest thou want t' horse?'. We still had it, an' I said no. And he selled it, it went for killing like. 'Twas a good horse an' all. **Tom Sedgwick** b.1917

And then there were tractors

Tractors were only just coming in and Mr Dinsdale was quite a progressive type of chap and he was the first one to have a tractor in Dentdale. And actually he was the first chap in Dentdale to manage his farm without horses. He did away with horses and we did everything by tractor. A lot of people had a tractor and a horse, which they still do, but we did away with the horses and did it all by tractors. **Fred Taylor** b.1927

We'd two sledges pulled by horse. We cut bracken and bedding rushes with a scythe in the early days, then we got an Allen auto-scythe. Then we got a little grey Fergie [Ferguson tractor], well that was like going to heaven, oh it revolutionised the situation. I could drive it the moment it came. **Dick Harrison** b.1934

On this farm here [Needle House, Uldale, Ravenstonedale] we went on farming until 1955 and we used horses throughout, but many other people by then were using tractors, those little grey Ferguson tractors, and a lot of the machinery they used that would have been simply towed by horses now had draw bars put on and were attached to tractors, which wasn't terribly efficient but that was the way it started out. So, the major change was this gradual changeover to tractor-based farming as opposed to horse-based and now, of course, that is virtually complete. **Helga Frankland** b.1920

> *I took the last horse back to Kirkby Stephen auction and was glad to see the last of it*

I liked the horse and bringing the hay to the barn, I liked haymaking very well… I liked it better when we got a tractor and I could roll around the field. **Betty Hartley** b.1913

Everybody loved horses but I didn't, I did not like working with them and I loved the tractors when they came, I would guess about 1950s, and it took me father three years to make his mind up which kind to get. We were pushing him all the time to buy a tractor, and I took the last horse back to Kirkby Stephen auction on the 24th of September to sell it and was glad to see the last of it and me father always said if we got a tractor we would break all the land up an' smash the drains in, because of course stone drains then were only about two foot six deep and he was absolutely right and that year was the wettest summer we'd ever had. I took that horse to Kirkby Stephen an' I came back into the hay field, we're still haytiming an' we carried on until about the middle of October, and the last crop grew back into the ground, we never did finish. We got this tractor, we broke all the drains as father said we would, we 'ad ruts must a' been two foot deep an' he was not very pleased with us and our tractor! But that was the change, we never went back to horses…

It was a David Brown 25 and the Ferguson had come in and me uncle next door 'ad got a Ferguson, so father had to make 'is mind up. We said we didn't want a Ferguson, we wanted a David Brown. We 'ad a lot of battles over it, verbal battles but nice ones, but in the end we prevailed an' we got one an' we bought it from George Mounsey in Sedbergh. We bought the tractor with a mid-mounted cutter bar and a hay sweep and it was £509 and the registration was MWX 803, I can still remember that! **David Hutchinson** b.1920

Then as now, dales folk were inventive – and frugal – so the old machinery was adapted to work with the new.

After the war Harry Ferguson of course invented the Ferguson tractor and most of the farmers had double 'orse machines pulled by two 'orses. Now Harry Tallon invented a contraption, you could alter a double 'orse mowing machine with a lever to lift the bed so we used to put hitches on for the tractor with a lever and I used to go round to Harry Tallon's [King's Square, Sedbergh] and blow the bellows so that he could make these hitches for tractors… In 1947 my father bought the first brand-new tractor, a Ferguson tractor, it cost £331 and father spent £1000. He got a sweep and a tractor, a mowing machine, a plough, and the whole cabooch cost £1000. **Leslie Robinson** b.1930

You used to have to nurse this old Ford Fergie along, it only had three gears, but then we bought a cutting machine for it but it wasn't a proper cutting machine like tractors have nowadays, it was a horse drawn cutting machine. Me dad modified it so instead of a horse pulling it the tractor pulled it but mother had to sit on it to pull the handle to lift it up when you got to a corner, and the actual cutting blade was driven by the metal wheels, it wasn't power driven or anything. **Garth Steadman** b.1945

I rather fancied having my own Fergie when we moved into Hobsons [Cowgill], so I bought a second-hand (or probably tenth-hand) one from Johnnie Akrigg at Ewegales. I'd never driven a tractor in my life, and was a bit disconcerted to find it had no brakes, so you had to rely on the gears. After a bit of practice I drove it up to Acre, probably the highest farm in Dentdale, with one of the steepest, bendiest tracks, and a deep ravine at the side. Then I had to get it down. After a few yards it

was running away with me. I couldn't get it into bottom gear and had to cling on for dear life as it raced down the hill, round the bends, bouncing over the rocks. Near the bottom, when I reckoned I must be travelling at the speed of sound, I managed to swing it off the track and into the field, where it eventually came to a halt. Next day I asked Johnnie if he'd buy it back. He did – and saved my life!
David Boulton b.1935

Plats, pikes, cocks and kemmins

On a small farm a machine was jus' run with one 'orse in shafts but a bigger farm, well, there was much more t' do, then you'd two 'orses to draw a machine an' they set out a *setting* maybe of two or three acres you'd mow at once, but yer only 'ad enough so that you could cope with it. If t' weather was fine then you would 'ave another settin' comin' on but you would 'ave one ready almost, gettin' towards hay, you would 'ave them comin' on in rotation. If there were any hedge sides, or what we call dykes or braes, we children had to scrape all these bankings down an' then carry it t' up on t' top so that it could get mixed up… An' if they 'adn't really time t' get it all in, an' it was like rain, they would put it into a little stack, little *stooks* as you would say, little *pikes* we used t' call them. Then if it didn't rain much next day they would go an' lead it in. You see, it was a good safe way of protecting

---

DIALECT TERMS

Many of the farming terms used in this chapter will be unfamiliar to all but local people and those who study regional dialect. They belong to a spoken rather than a written language and though precise definitions may vary they illustrate the high level of expertise needed for successful 'haytiming'. Farmers mew, *or* mowed, *the hay and divided the area of work to be done into* sets *or* settings, *and* plats; *they* scaled (spread) *the hay and if rain threatened they made it into various sized heaps called* pikes, foot cocks *and* jockey cocks. *They raked the hay into* windrows *and gathered armfuls or* kemmins *[from 'combing in'] for loading onto* sledges, *or* sleds, *where land was steep. They led the hay to the* shippon (barn) *where a* mooer *stacked it in the* moo. *In days before mechanical balers they made a* dess *or* dessel, *the equivalent of a bale, cut from the heap with a knife. These words, many of Norse origin, are key to understanding haytime processes and some are still used today by the older generation.*

your 'ay from gettin' wet through. But if it were showery, if it wasn't ready for 'ay, you would go wi' yer rake an' make little *cocks* an' then t' air would blow through it, yer see. If it were like for rain yer made two big 'eaps, put one on top o' t' other, an' they were what were called '*jockey cocks*', that were a protection so that if it did come a shower it ran off the outside. **Cissy Middleton** b.1914

Once you've got [the hay] dry you need to row it into *windrows*. Windrows were made using pairs of people turning their row towards one another to form a thicker row than the turned row. Each person would be able to gather two turnings so a windrow would be four turnings thick. Each windrow had to be a sled-width apart so the horse and sled didn't trample on the hay… You didn't necessarily mow round a whole field, you mowed a suitable *plat*. You did a section and then you fitted these sections together. **Helga Frankland** b.1920

I think it was me brother, 'e was leadin' 'orses an' we were up on t' high meadow an' you had t' go along t' rows an' then turn in t' go round in between what we called two plats, that was two rows where you were leadin' from these plats, an' when it turned round it caught somethin' on this 'orse's leg an' it took off! An' this little lad, 'e would maybe be ten, eleven, something like that, an' I can see that t' this day, this 'orse jus' goin' wild, as fast as ever it could! This little lad was hangin' on by its *hames* [wood or metal pieces by which the harness is attached to the collar]. But eventually it shook 'im off, dropped 'im, with it gallopin', but e' came to no harm! Eventually me dad got rid o' that 'orse, it were too dangerous. **Cissy Middleton** b.1914

A *kemmin* was when you ran it [the hay] along with the rake. Say you were loading a sledge, you would run it along, put your arm over an' pick it up, that bundle, an' that was a kemmin an' you put that on the sledge. **Kenneth Cragg** b.1936

When yer were loadin' a sled yer used to get a rake an' yer made a kemmin with runnin' yer rake up [the row] an' then gettin' a big armful, get as much as you can, then oop yer went an' tipped it up fer whoever's on t' cart, an' there it built up that way. Yer 'adn't jus' t' throw it on any way, you turned it so it was neat and tidy. **Cissy Middleton** b.1914

Very occasionally we made a stack, the whole idea is that it sheds rain. A proper stack meant to stand in the field is put on *staddles*, a sort of wooden framework, which you make your stack on. **Helga Frankland** b.1920

You make a row of hay by *casting*, what they call casting in. You make your row, then you turn the rake the wrong side up an' you run it along an' push the hay in front of you, and then you turn the rake back over, reach forward as far as you can, an' you pull it back on to your feet an' that makes a *foot cock*, an' then you run another one, if you were going to make them to last better or dry better you run another one and put it on top, and the main idea was it left the land to dry around the cock, then next day you broke them out with a fork and shook it all out on to the dry clean land. **Kenneth Cragg** b.1936

The worst thing was that when you had made these hay cocks they had to be spread out again and we used to hate doing that because my father was very strict about not letting us use a fork. It was for safety really and we had to do it by hand. It was effective, it did help to dry a lot, but we didn't like doing it. **Betty Harper** b.1920

There's two types of *piking*. You can make pikes, which is heaps of hay, or you can pike a field, which is cutting grass round the dyke banks. **Kenneth Cragg** b.1936

> *You could lie on your back, put your feet against the rafters, and push the hay down*

Stacking the moo

There would be a *forker-up* and a *mooer*, and the forker-up had one of these long forks and forked up variable sizes, depending on his strength and ambition, and it was amazing what some people could fork up. So then the mooer received it on top and the great idea was they had a short fork, or possibly just arms, you certainly hadn't room when the moo got high [near the roof of the barn]. And you scattered it round evenly and you always trod it down well, especially round the walls because that, of course, is where it stuck! And the great thing was, it must be even. And if it were in a barn where you could lead the horse in, alongside the moo, well, then of course, you got a front *dressing*. The man on the ground did the dressing and kept it straight, otherwise there was an awful tendency for it to slope in, but if it was forked in through a forking hole, of course then you'd got walls all the way round and it was slightly less skilled to do that. And if you were the mooer, when it got really near the top, you could lie on your back, put your feet against the rafters and push, you see, because they kept it coming, and you say 'It's nearly full!' 'Oh no, it isn't!' the forker-up would say! And of course you'd got to deal with it until he agreed that it really was full…

Some buildings had a *sunk moo*. There was a *byre* on the right with cows tied up, facing in towards the centre of the barn, and *foddering holes* where the hay could be put in from ground level in front of the cows and then spread out in the space enlarged into a loft above the byre. However, often these byres were on hillsides and the horse was taken in at loft level to unload with enough space left to remove the horse, which was then filled afterwards. The entire byre, cow level and loft, had to be completely full…

You cut hay in blocks using a hay knife. If it needed to be carried somewhere a *dess* was made, which was generally a cubic yard of hay and a cord put round it to carry it to a field or even to another farm. Some people bought a barn of hay and it would be cut out into desses, loaded onto something and brought home. **Helga Frankland** b.1920

'If you put it in too green an' it sweat too much you got a barn fire'

I was trying to save a gate going off into a *sink moo*, a sink moo is where the hay comes in in steep ground, on the top. You bring your hay in there and then it drops down so there's no forking up. It would be, what, about a ten foot drop, and I was putting a gate down and I was trying to save the gate from tipping on one end, in a hurry of course, not paying attention, and I fell and slid down by the side of the gate and broke me arm when I hit the ground. **Myles Jackson** b.1928

When they got it up on to the moo they shook it all out again, they didn't leave it in them kemmins, you spread it all out even an' that was supposed to be that it would sweat better, 'cos you'd got to let the sweat come out an' go out of the top. If you put it in too green an' it sweat too much an' get hot then you got a barn fire. It did happen in the valley quite a bit. **Kenneth Cragg** b.1936

When the sun wouldn't shine

Well one year we tried all ways. We'd put a new barn up, about 1954, and we'd no hay in it. We 'ad to sell some cows off that we should have kept, it was such a bad time. You couldn't get it in. It was rain every day. And floods. Every two or three days you were in floods. There was twelve acres never did get mown. **Jim Middleton** b.1913

One year it rained and rained and the last plat hadn't been mown and it got into, oh, late August, early September and we just sort of thought, well, we'll just have to leave it unmown. Well then the weather took up so we got all our things out again (they had been put away into lofts and places for the winter) and mowed it off and turned it into hay and so… well at least it was a crop! And it wasn't too bad because it hadn't grown an awful lot, the grass wasn't that long, it didn't get laid the way it does because it was herb-rich, shortish grass anyway. Lots of lovely wild flowers in it and very attractive kind of hay for animals to eat. These flowers, as opposed to grass, have deeper roots, you see, and they bring up minerals, and whether that's why stock like it I don't know, but they certainly do and they'll eat that rather than a heap of rag-grass and clover any day! **Helga Frankland** b.1920

Haytime refreshments

You made a lot of haverbread [oatcake] before haytime to help things along. On a backstone. It's a round flat pan… and it would be on t' fire, you see. [Mother] would mek a good stack and put it into newspaper, keep it and then when they went with it out into t' hayfield they took it buttered and a piece o' cheese. **Bessie Mason** b.1911

We often used to take a meal outside. People used to come to help sometimes, so we used to take a basket with food in and a can with tea in and go and sit on a sledge or somewhere and have something to eat outside. 'Ten o'clocks' we used to call it, ten o'clock we used to take a meal out, then come back to the house for lunch, we called it dinner then, that would be the main meal. Then it was back to the field right away, there wasn't much break in haytime, it was all go then. Hay, never silage! **Mary Cowperthwaite** b.1924

> *Bacon sandwiches, 'ten o' clocks', cheese and a can of tea – no time to come in for a meal*

Sometimes breakfast was carried out t' them because they couldn't loose out their 'orses if they 'adn't finished. They would take the breakfast out, you know, even if it were a bacon sandwich. Then breakfast in t' 'ouse, we would all jus' try t' get our work done an' then be out in t' field by eight or nine o'clock, even t' womenfolks 'cos every pair o' hands was needed. An' then you used t' 'ave a 'ten o'clock', a bit o' bread an' cheese an' a can o' tea an' a biscuit, an' that would always be carried out an' into t' field for a 'ten o'clock'. An' then midday it used to be more or less sandwiches, boiled ham an' some sandwiches, an' maybe an apple pasty, something like that. But it was allus carried out because there was too much time wasted comin' in fer a meal. You couldn' waste any time on a farm, every minute was vital an' precious because if it looked like rain yer couldn't bother about t'meal, yer'd t' think about yer 'ay, an' get it!...

After we'd 'ad our dinner you would start work again an' three o'clock would be generally yer teatime, someone would nip away an' make yer tea, bread an' jam an' cake, another big can o' tea, an' sit on a sled out in t' field an' jus' 'ave a picnic. Oh, it was grand! An' t' bus would be goin' up an' they'd all be waving at us, you know! Many a time visitors come an' would jus' come an' talk t' us. It was like a novelty to them. Some youngsters would come an' well near spend all their 'olidays with us, even parents got t' come an' they would all sit down an' 'ave a cup of tea with us… Six o'clock it was thrown down fer milkin' time, an' then as soon as t' milkin' was finished there was another meal made an' sometimes it were porridge, tea an' biscuits or cheese, whatever we 'ad, an' then out t' work again an' maybe' till…oh, you'd be at it till ten or eleven o'clock, whatever, leadin' if it was leadin' or preparin' fer another day or whatever. An' that was a full day's work! **Cissy Middleton** b.1914

My father used to buy us a nine gallon barrel of beer from the Dragon at Dent. Just at haytime, t' keep us at work. **Jack Middleton** b.1921

Helping the neighbours

If anybody finished soon they used to go and help somebody else, that often 'appened when it was such 'ard work. **Mary Ellison** b.1909

As soon as we finished haytime, if there was anybody else needed any help, away we 'ad to go, and help anybody else out. You don't see a great lot of that now unless it's a payment, isn't it? It's all pay, it has to be paid today. We 'adn't to think about that, you know, we'd just simply to go and help. No, we would go, like, up as far as Tofts [Dent Crag, above Gawthrop] where there was some elderly people… And Bower Bank, there was a couple there with nothing… You just didn't stick to your own family. If you could see to giving anybody a hand to get the crops in, then away you went. **Cissy Middleton** b.1914

CHAPTER 8

Women's work

On the farm – Household chores –
Wash days and smoothing irons – Feeding the family –
Rug-making, sewing and knitting – Earning a living from home –
Going out to work – Women's Institute

*I*n this chapter women tell how they did their share of farm work as well as feeding their families and running their households. In times when social and medical services were scarce women took on roles as carers and nurses, often voluntarily. Many young girls got jobs as general home helps on leaving school, a few found work in shops and offices. Despite their busy lives many made time for voluntary work in the community. A woman's work was never done!

On the farm

Till Bob left school I helped George [Mary's husband]. I was determined to learn to milk, so I managed that, and then you'd have to feed all the calves and then you'd have to run in and get some breakfast. You'd have buildings up here [at Far Helks, Dentdale] and buildings further down, so you had to go to those. You'd to go all round your hens… well it nearly took you while dinner time before you got all that seen to. I used to be popping in to put a bit of dinner on and running out again! **Mary Ellison** b.1909

I was a hen keeper and I produced eggs, sold them to the local shops and that's how I earned my living at home. We farmed for fifty years together. That's what my husband wanted to do. It was joint partnership, yes. Oh I did anything, I used to drive things about, I used to work the machinery in the haymaking field and that. **Betty Hartley** b.1913

First winter we 'ad, you know, we'd a lot o' snow, but I remember going out to some outer barns to feed cattle in a morning while 'e [husband Jim] was milking, 'cos we'd no man then. We'd Foulsyke and Low Haycote ground [Gawthrop], which was like two farms, so we'd quite a bit of work… I know I've had to stand with Jim and rub a cow to keep it calm after a first calf and they were uneasy. I've had to stand and stroke one at midnight while he's been milking it, and all that sort of thing. **Cissy Middleton** b.1914

Oh! I 'ad me hens! Three different hen houses t' go an' tek a great big bucket of soft stuff ready, in the mornings. No wonder me back's quaking a bit now! Oh, and I loved me sheep. I used t' look forward t' the clipping time, an' I could darn me stockins after that 'cos oh, me hands were lovely an' greasy! **Jenny Kiddle** b.1918

The stone quarries up here [Deepdale], the Mason quarries, the man would work up there and the woman would run the farm. The man would help out a lot but if they were working on the railway up Cowgill the womenfolk would run the farm and they'd go full time, eight hours, on the rail. Of course a lot of women milked, just as good as men at milkin'. The really heavy work the man would do it, but they would mostly have a full time job at the quarry and the railway. **Miley Taylor** b.1923

> *Every day had its job. And Sunday was the day of rest*

Household chores

Every week you'd have a full baking day and it took all day. And you'd have a big washing day on a Monday, and iron, 'cos you'd iron with a flat iron… And then you'd have a day for doing your bedrooms out and a day for cleaning up downstairs. Then you'd a day, afternoon at mending, 'cos men's clothes took a lot of mending then, they did! And I don't know what else, you always had a very full week, I always seemed to 'ave. Then every night you sat down and cleaned eggs for an hour or two. **Mary Ellison** b.1909

Usually Saturdays was scrubbing out day when you went through the rooms and scrubbed the flags down. Monday would be washing day, and Tuesday would be another day for something else, and Wednesday would be a baking day and Thursday would be a room day. And Friday would be maybe churning day and Saturday would be t' cleaning up day. Aye, every day had its job. And Sunday was the day of rest...

It was a big house was Olmonds [Gawthrop] and what I used to dread most was when it come to spring cleaning. I'd all these curtains to take down and they were usually all let in with lace. And all t' blinds were like stiff white blinds with crotchet on t' bottom. And we used to have to take 'em off these rollers and wash 'em and starch 'em, and then put them back up again. And I used to carry that on till I think maybe wartime when we'd to start blacking out and we'd to put something black up. I think that would do away with a lot of that, but oh it was hard work, was that! I used to dread it, 'cos there was about seventeen windows all through, and there was a lot of work. But anyway, I was strong enough to do it. **Cissy Middleton** b.1914

My mother always had to work hard bringing up the children and looking after the house. She never went out to work for anybody else because she was always busy at home with the [ten] children, with the family. **Albert Fothergill** b.1923

Washdays and smoothing irons

We always washed on a Monday. We 'adn't a tap then, there's a gill at t' back field and they would have to carry water from there when it was washing day. There was a dolly tub and dolly legs an' an old fashioned big mangle what you twined around. And they allus had a big dish with blue in, all the white things had to go through this blue. It was a big day. We'd have to get up a bit earlier, filling t' wash boiler and lighting t' fire, a coal fire an' wood an' that, yes they were oft out for sticking. Thursday was baking, allus a Thursday. They were on all t' day because they baked bread and teacakes and scones and fruit pasties an' cake, ginger cake or something. Every week, yeah. **Mary Allen** b.1923

"The electric med a different world altogether!"

Tuesday was ironing day and we used charcoal. We had to get some charcoal into a wire pan and put it on the fire and then put it into the charcoal iron, and then we had to keep filling it up and blowing it and heat it up. It was quite a business. **Mary Cowperthwaite** b.1924

Before we got wash boilers it was really awful 'cos we'd all the water t' carry. When I was at Dee Cottage [Cowgill] we'd t' go up t' road an' down in t' beck an' get the water, there was a well under t' road, we got it there. No, no runnin' water in any house till I was in me forties… Everything, you'd t' carry it in. Nobody knows what it's like when yer have a farm and you've all yer water t' heat fer calves an' everything in a boiler beside the fire. I'd use mebbe a dozen buckets a day.

You always seemed t' be runnin' up t' road fer a couple o' buckets! **Mary Ellison** b.1909

There was a tank at the house end for rain water, quite a big grey tank, zinc would it be? I think we would have a tap that that came out of in the kitchen, into the sink. And we used to go down into the wood with buckets and there was the well, the spring down there, which was a square, rusty looking box, a bit bigger than a biscuit tin, set into the hillside. The water came out of it in a spout and filled your bucket and it was wet all round, and then you went up again, it was quite steep and you'd to carry your bucket up and you'd go through that little gate in the front hedge, outside the front door. **Freda Trott** b.1919

Electricity med all the difference in the world! You 'ad this light, you'd to fill paraffin lamps which are stinking things… I 'ad one of the thrills of my life when I washed with an electric washer, a twin tub. We 'ad to have big washings with t' lads, and ironing! Well there was a flat iron and there was a box iron that you put the heaters in the fire to get red hot, and there was a charcoal iron and then there was this polishing iron, oval. Father always wore these very white stiff collars, it was a work of art doing them. He'd go to t' auction in a collar and tie, and Sundays. Oh, the electric med a different world altogether! Vacuum cleaners were grand, they were very light, that made all the difference in the world, better than beating carpets! Life changed altogether! No dust! **Elizabeth Middleton** b.1915

Feeding the family

We used t' get a ten stone bag [of flour] about every month. But there would be, oh, at least two stone put into a big tin for our bread because we usually made about twenty four loaves in a day when

In the 1926 coal strike I'd pick up dried cow claps to heat oven

we 'ad a proper bakin' day, an' it took us an hour t' knead our bread up. You've got yer oven hot an' you would start, when yer got yer bread med up, that 'ad t' rise at least fer an hour an' more. When that was rising yer med yer pastry an med yer apple pies or plum pies or rhubarb or whatever you were mekin', an' yer used t' get them in first. An' you would mek a pasty for every day, 'cause we only baked once a week, an' yer med enough pasties an' Eccles cake, an' sometimes if we run short we'd mek a sad cake in t' frying pan over t' fire, it's like pastry without any fruit in, and yer rolled it out into rounds an' popped it into your greased frying pan an' then when it got browned underneath jus' turned it over, an' they were good! A bit o' butter on! Lots of folk would 'ave a sad cake fer a drinking at elevenses. **Cissy Middleton** b.1914

On baking day me mother used to make twenty six loaves of bread a day and it being an open fire we used to cut lengths of wood approximately six foot long, and she used to have a chair set out in the kitchen with the end of the logs on the chair and the other end in the fire and as it burned down you just kept pushing the chair forward and that kept the fire going all day for baking day. **Kenneth Cragg** b.1936

In 1926 miners went on strike and then t' coal man went, there was no coal, railways stopped and t' auction, everything stopped. It was a lovely summer an' we used to have to bake our own bread and my mother and I used to go out into t' front paddock and pick up dried cow claps to heat t' oven. **Bessie Mason** b.1911

We used to preserve eggs, because when there was a glut of butter and eggs Mr. Tony Edmondson [shop-keeper] just couldn't get rid of all these eggs and butter, and we could buy a shilling a dozen for eggs, and about a shilling a pound for butter. And the eggs were preserved in something called 'water glass' [sodium silicate], and you could buy special buckets with a basket, like a large chip basket, and put the eggs in and then lower it into this 'water glass'. They were just really used for cooking. I don't think anybody would boil them. And the butter was wrapped in muslin and preserved in brine. [My mother] also made jams. I can remember stirring and stirring! **Marjorie Middleton** b.1913

My grandmother was a great jam maker and they had fruit trees down the garden and she would make redcurrant jelly and all sorts, blackcurrant and all sorts of jams. It makes me mouth water to think about those good jams! **Freda Trott** b.1919

For supper we'd maybe have porridge, 'boddish' as they called it, oatmeal porridge.

Or you might have bread pudding, bread and sugar and milk. Good! There was **'Cutting up, clip, clip, clipping away making hearthrugs'** nowt wasted, lass! Crusts of bread, a bit of currant in or something sometimes, yeah. That was special! **Miley Taylor** b.1923

We grew most of our own vegetables but of course them days they were seasonal, you couldn't keep them. Mother used to do an awful lot of bottling, bottled fruit, we used to pick hundredweights of blackberries. I was so sick of blackberries, we'd blackberry pie and blackberry jam and blackberry pasty, everything was blackberries at that time of year, but when she bottled them of course you could then use them in winter. She used to bottle them in Kilner jars. **Kenneth Cragg** b.1936

Rug-making, sewing and knitting

I used t' make me hearthrugs. Cuttin' up, clip, clip, clipping away night an' day. Made a good price of them as well! I made £12 for one of mine, an' it was a good one, too! Length of the hearth 'ere [3 foot]. **Jenny Kiddle** b.1918

We used to get up early in the morning, it'd be six or seven o'clock, to make these rugs. Oh quite a few hours a day, we used to make all the rugs we had. I used to clip up and peg, you know. You see we'd no television or wireless and we used to take turns at reading from a magazine to each other while the other worked. We made our own designs, we just drew on them what we fancied doing. I've always loved making rugs. **Betty Hartley** b.1913

It was a job cutting it up [for rag rugs]. Men used to wear a lot of fushan [fustian] trousers, knee britches as we used to call 'em. Well, you washed them and then took t' best parts out and probably outlined a border or something like that. And you used to have plenty of black, patterned hessian, stamped hessian. And you used to make 'em really pretty with doing all your colours…

We would buy a ten stone bag o' flour every month an' it used t' come from

Sedbergh with horse an' cart, in a big, white bag an' it 'ad 'Snowflake' written on it, it was Snowflake flour, very good flour! But those bags were allus kept an' made use of. If it was a good quality bag they med it into pillowcases, we've had them med into little bits o' vests fer wearing as children, they were med fer bed covers. After they were bleached they took all this lettering away and they were snow-white an' they were med a lot of use of! **Cissy Middleton** b.1914

The sacks, well, all the cattle feed came in so we'd plenty of hessian sacks. The good sacks we used to use for making rugs and mother used to put them on the frame and then we'd make the peg rugs. The white flour sacks were always bleached and used for sheets 'cos you couldn't buy sheets in wartime. I can still remember the outline of Pattisons' flour on me sheets and who was the other? One from Liverpool, Rank Hovis, we used to have their sheets. **Kenneth Cragg** b.1936

> *People still talk about my vanilla slices. I baked 60 a week for Sedbergh market*

Oh auntie was always knitting, sewing or something, so was me grandmother. She would do beautiful fine work. I had two beautiful tablecloths, they were too nice to use, to plonk tea on. I gave them to Howgill church, very deep hand knitted lace. Oh they were never idle, never ever sat doing nothing. **Freda Trott** b.1919

Saturday night we did a lot of darning. Everybody wore woollen socks and we had a big darning basket and we sat round darning. We knit a lot, cardigans, jumpers and socks. We always had some knitting on the go. **Mary Cowperthwaite** b.1924

Earning a living from home

Mother went up to Lea Gate [Lea Yeat, Cowgill], we took a house up there, and she started a shop. She was a milliner, was mother, and she kept going wi' meking hats till she got enough money to start a shop, and kept buying a little bit o' something, and that's how she did. And I lived up there till I went to Dee Cottage [Cowgill]. Grandma had a shop there and I stopped with her till we were married. **Mary Ellison** b.1909

We used to make about £40 worth of stuff for Sedbergh market. Oh, the market was important. I dressed hens and turkeys and things, and I baked. People talk about my vanilla slices now! I used to do about sixty a week at one time. Yes it was quite useful income. I'd make biscuits and all, I used to make ginger fairlings, they were popular, people liked it. You've got to please your customers, you know. I used to make apple pies, jams, marmalade. Hundreds and hundreds of pounds of marmalade I made for the market. I also took eggs, quite a good number, perhaps five or six dozens, it was my pin money. You see we didn't go out to work in those days, you worked with what you had at home. **Betty Hartley** b.1913

Mother was a very good sewer, she made lots of clothes. There was a Miss Benson, she used to sew for mother and there was Cissy Greenwood, she was a sewer, to make us underwear and all kinds of things. Lots of people sewing, oh yes. **Elizabeth Middleton** b.1915

Norman's mother [Jenny's mother-in-law] used to keep the shop, in the farmhouse [Holme Hill, Cowgill] in the pantry. She used t' sell butter. She'd get butter in an' of course she made it as well with 'er churn. At 'oliday times they used t' 'ave good trade sellin' all 'er stuff. She used t' bake as well. **Jenny Kiddle** b.1918

Going out to work

[My mother's] uncle was postmaster in Dent and [my mother] did a postal walking round. She did a long way, she started at Mill Beck and walked up to Gawthrop and up to Pease Gill House, which is no longer there, and across to Combe and Tofts, right down to the end of the dale, and then back up the other side of the dale and up to Hall House and High Hall and back home again. People didn't get many letters in those days, some places she might only go to once a week… After her uncle died she took over as postmistress. **Marjorie Middleton** b.1913

My parents went to Sedbergh National School as children and mother stayed on as a pupil teacher under Mr Dennis. She was paid a shilling a week as a pupil teacher. Then she studied and was certificated from Durham University. She stayed at Sedbergh National School, which is now the telephone exchange, until she was married, and then they went to Halifax and mother taught all round Halifax schools, supply work. And she always said that was what had enabled her to take the headship at Howgill school where there was about thirty children then. She died in 1927 when I was eight… I started teaching piano when I was sixteen. By the time I was eighteen I had about thirty. The most pupils I ever had was forty eight a week. I always enjoyed it. I only gave it up when I was two months off being seventy five. **Freda Trott** b.1919

After leaving school I went to look after a little boy, Mrs Ward's son, nine months old, up Joss Lane [Sedbergh]. I was there for maybe eighteen months. And then I went to Jacksons to work as a sort of general assistant. When Mr Greasley started this idea of making furniture polish, Jackson's furniture polish, I used to bottle that and label it. That was done at the Bull yard, in the anteroom up the Bull yard. Yes, I liked shop work. **Doris Waller** b. 1920

"Ten shillings a year, you didn't get rich fast!"

She [mother] had trained as a nurse and worked away from Sedbergh for a while and then come back to Sedbergh as the district nurse. After she married, while I was a small child she ran this house [Hylands] as a maternity home. **George Handley** b.1937

Me mum and me aunt used to go when anyone 'ad a baby for a fortnight, 'cos you stopped in bed a fortnight then, an' they would do t' work an' look after any more children that was there. They would get paid I think. And if anybody died they used to go an' wash 'em an' lay them out. **Mary Allen** b.1923

I kept old graves clean, Mrs Hicks's graves, they're all white ones up near the riverside. I got ten shillings a year for that. She sent wreaths at Christmas and I used to t' put wreaths on an' kept it cut. You didn't get rich fast, did you? **Mary Ellison** b.1909

I was at home till about I was fifteen, then I went out for a days' work. That's what you did then. Two and six a day. That's what we got. Different peoples' houses, a washing day or baking day. **Mary Allen** b.1923

I went to Poulton le Fylde to look after two little boys. I was seventeen. It wasn't my decision, my parents arranged it, but they were relatives. Both the parents worked on the railway. I think I got paid about ten shillings a week. **Mary Cowperthwaite** b.1924

I went on to John Laing Construction, the M6 motorway. Yes, that was '69. That was in the process [of being built]. I was secretary to the project manager there. When I went it was at Lowgill. I always say that I built the motorway – along with 999 others! They worked hard and they played hard, they really did… I left there and I went to the Bank of Europe, and at that time computers were just coming in and everything was being centralised and I was there till 1979 in Kendal. Then they closed that and I went to Forward Trust, the financing arm of the Midland Bank, and I were there till I retired in 1985. Yes, I've been made redundant three times altogether, and actually I've been very lucky because one slotted in with the other all the way along the line. I was very fortunate, I don't think you could actually do it today. **Kitty Howard** b. *c*1925

In those days a lot of people sent their washing to the laundry down Guldrey. [Sedbergh]. I once went inside this laundry and it was very hot and steamy, and quite a lot of ladies worked there, washing these clothes in big drums and then drying them and ironing them. **Peter Iveson** b.1938

In the very early days mum used to work at the Sedbergh laundry and after that she used to clean at one of the pubs in Sedbergh, the Golden Lion – it's now The Dalesman. I got a job in Timothy Whites in Kendal, my first proper job, I was about sixteen… Then I got a job helping to run the Sedbergh Post Office. You got to know all the local people, the farmers in particular – they were a right laugh! **Judith Allison** b.1954

The Women's Institute

I joined the WI a few months after it was started, over fifty years ago. And we've done all kinds of things in the past. We competed in the drama festival at Kendal and the Mary Wakefield Festival. Off and on I was president for sixteen years, just whenever they couldn't get a president. I've worked for the WI all me time it's been going. And we helped to cater for the Dent gala and do all sorts of public work. It's a very useful body is the WI. **Betty Hartley** b.1913

Well, I was one of t' founder members of t' Women's Institute [in Dent]. I was one of t' first to go. There wasn't so many of us then. Miss Steele came from Kendal t' tell you all about it an' what was expected of a meetin' and 'ow you'd t' run it, an' then old Mrs Ellison, she was t' main leader and she started off to help us to sew, and I remember cutting these pyjamas out for my eldest little lad, he'd be seven or eight maybe and I made him a pair of pyjamas under Mrs Ellison's supervision. It would have been 1944 to '45 or round there… Everybody was asked t' write a motto down, an' Sarah Hartley won it with 'Unity is Strength', an' as a watchword it was quite a good thing, wasn't it? **Cissy Middleton** b.1914

CHAPTER 9

Hearth and home

Traditional houses – Baths and lavatories –
Water supplies – Heating the home: peat and coal –
Lamps and candle light – Gas – Electricity –
Wartime prefabs – Social housing – Sheltered housing –
Offcomers, the new property owners

Home for many was a traditional dales farmhouse or cottage, often dating back to the seventeenth or eighteenth century though altered by successive generations. Few had hot and cold water laid on till well into the twentieth century, bathrooms as we know them were rare and indoor lavatories were by no means the norm. Sleeping arrangements were often cramped, particularly where families were large, and children were used to sharing a bed.

Traditional houses

We lived at Ravenstonedale until I was fourteen. There were three bedrooms. My mother and dad had a biggish bedroom and there was always a cot in there, and the boys' bedroom was a long one, and there'd be three of them sleeping in there, and then the girls' bedroom, there was often three or four of us in bed… We went to live at Garsdale Hall in 1944. There was a big kitchen and a flagged floor and a sink, reddish brown, I know dad used to sharpen his knives on it, and there's one tap there. The water wasn't very good, it came from across the road. It must have come from a spring but there wasn't so much of it sometimes, so we were rather limited. And we had a big table down the middle, it was a big kitchen, and we had a cooler for the milk. Round at back there was a set boiler for washing days, with a fireplace underneath. It was called an 'L' boiler 'cause it went right round the back of the fireplace, and at the other side there was an oven where we used to bake our bread and everything…

There was a big pantry with shelves round and a stone floor. Then you'd turn left along a passageway and then left again into quite a big living room. And there was an old-fashioned fireplace, a black-leaded fireplace, and we had a table and chairs, we had to have quite a lot of chairs because there were a lot of us to sit round the table. I think we had a form at the back of the table for some of us to sit on, and there was, well you call them a couch now, in front of the window, a couple of old easy chairs at either side of the fireplace, and a pegged rug, and we had what we called oil cloth on the floor, you could sweep it up and mop it. From there you went through another door into the front passage which led from the front door, and there was a door opposite into quite a big, what we called the sitting room. We did have another sitting room, it was a best room, we had a three-piece suite and we used to have parties sometimes of a night in wintertime and people used to come and so we used to use that room then. And then you went upstairs and at the top there was a room at either side. One was just a box-room place, and the other we used for having a good wash and things like that, we had a wash-stand in it, and then you went into another passageway and there was four bedrooms. The one nearest Sedbergh was a big room and we used to call it the dance room because long ago they used to have dances in that room, they said, because the floor wasn't straight, it wasn't level. And then there were another three bedrooms, big ones at either side and smaller ones in the middle. So we had quite a lot of room there. We didn't hold dances or anything. It used to be a pub long ago did Garsdale Hall, but I don't know when. **Mary Cowperthwaite** b.1924

> *'No Hoovers, yer 'ad t' get down on yer 'ands and knees an' sweep!'*

It was a big house was Olmonds [Gawthrop]. There was oilcloth on the floor and wallpaper. They were all wallpapered, the rooms, an' usually a nice frieze put round. You know, it was p'raps not as modern as what it is today, but it did, you 'adn't Hoovers or anything, yer 'ad t' get down on yer 'ands an' knees an' sweep! Downstairs there was two sitting rooms. One, we called 'little room', if we wanted t' make a pegged 'earthrug or me mother wanted t' do some quilting, they would use this little sitting room for that purpose. There would be a fireplace put in an' there you'd set your frames up an' yer got on with yer work an' yer needn't t' cut [the threads] t' take it down. But the other one was a lovely room an' it 'ad two windows to it, right by t' roadside, an' it was very nicely furnished an' it was there for if you'd any visitors at all. An' when I was married me wedding presents were put in this little room…

We 'ad a lovely farm'ouse kitchen, an' all round t' sides was done wi' old oak from out of church. When they did away with a lot of box pews in t' centre of [Dent] church we must 'ave bought a lot of this old wood an' it was all panelled, all round, with this lovely oak, an' then at one corner there was a good double-doored cupboard let in t' wall, an' when we went there there was t' old range, big black range, an' in t' corner there was a water system an' I think that was boxed in was this tank where we'd t' water, an' then that fed in t' our boiler. It was our own water supply. An' from t' fireplace, boiler, they 'ad it made so that they could draw it from a tap out into t' back kitchen, which was a long kitchen, a good, long kitchen. An' there we 'ad a big pot rail, from bottom t' top, where you put things an' yer kept all yer crockery, an' bottom on t' floor, well, you usually kept yer bucket o' coal an' popped yer pile o' sticks fer t' mornin', an' shoes. An' yer 'ad a table t' set all yer pots on an' you'd yer sink, an' then you'd another corner with our separator, where we separated milk. **Cissy Middleton** b.1914

> *We had the old black range with the crane on top*

The original range at Deepdale Head was beautiful. We 'ad an open grate and it 'ad reckons [cranes] on and you could adjust how high the pan was above the fire. I don't know how we did it with an open fire, frying bacon and egg, we always had bacon and egg and porridge. We had a cold tap over the boiler, the boiler and our oven always had a separate fire. The door for the fire was right under the oven and it would 'old ten two-pound loaves. **Elizabeth Middleton** b.1915

We had the old black range with the crane over the top, me mother had what we today would call a cauldron, it was about two foot six deep and approximately two foot six across and all the washing was done in there over a black range, and then later on in the early 1950s we put a set boiler in the back kitchen. I remember them building that, we thought that was a wonderful thing. **Kenneth Cragg** b.1936

We arrived in Sedbergh by train [in 1943]. All our furniture had gone into store in Kendal and we were delivered with part of the furniture and all the family, meself, mum, Phyllis and Keith, and we went up by Coward's horse and cart in the dark! I can remember going over Longstone Fell with this huge moon shining on us. We were delivered to Low House Farm [Garsdale] by Dick Middleton. It was completely cold! There was only one bedroom so it had mum's double bed and the beds for the rest of us. But the floor wasn't level and with a little bit of jumping up and down you could get the beds to move away from the wall and run down into the centre, which used to amuse us but it didn't used to amuse me mum. Oh, it is a very old farm, is Low House. A lovely old house! You would call it nearly

Tudor style but quite a busy farm as well. It's still in the family. We burnt wood that was provided by Dick on the farm. It was just a big fireplace. The bedroom wasn't heated, it was just a case of hot water bottles, the stone ones, going in at about seven o'clock at night to warm the bed up. And Phyllis slept on her own but I slept with brother Keith so you kept yourself reasonably warm. The farm sitting room had the huge fire and oven and every Saturday Martha used to bake and then she'd come through and say to mum 'Yer can have the oven now'. So mum used to bake as well. And they used to have these lovely big homemade rugs, tag rugs as they called them, like a rag thing made with sack, and we used to be allowed to lay on that until our faces were bright red in front of the fire. **Bob Turner** b.1933

> *The ceilings were so low you had to bend down to get your shirt on*

I was born in Main Street, Dent, opposite where the blacksmith's shop was in Beech Hill. They've taken all the houses down now and our house was just a living room with a bit taken off for a kitchen, and a bedroom upstairs and a little bedroom at back agin' the staircase. Just imagine! **Mary Ellison** b.1909

The ceilings were that low, what would it be, six foot, and in those days a shirt didn't fasten up the front like a jacket, you pulled it over your head and then tied the top three buttons. Well, you'd to put your hands up in the air to get it on, you couldn't get it up 'cos the ceiling was so low you had to half bend down to get your shirt on… We married in 1950 and we lived with mother. [It was] only a little house, a bigger room and a smaller one, and we lived there until we got one of our own [in the railway cottages, Garsdale]. Things weren't very good. There was no electric in the houses, we'd no water in, we just had a little coal fire with an oven, an Aladdin lamp and paraffin. We had one tap fed sixteen houses and that was it. We caught rain in the water barrels and that was handy for women washing. There was no modern living then. **Dennis Abbott** b.1926

The household was fairly hectic because apart from my parents and seven children we had for a long time a Dr. Kersey as a guest in the house, so the whole house was fairly crowded. So what we had was a shed that was built outside in the garden and the two oldest boys slept and worked in the shed outside, and as Herbert left

Lawrence moved into the shed, but before I became an occupant of the shed we left that house. **David Hutchinson** b.1920

Baths and lavatories

We 'adn't a bathroom then, we just had a 'bungalow bath' they called 'em, tin baths. Went certain nights when certain of 'em 'ad gone to bed. You wonder how you did now, don't you? You had to get all this hot water for t' bath like, but we'd have fireside boiler, wouldn't we? **Mary Allen** b.1923

You had to carry hot water up to the bathroom and I think the bath was fixed in what is now the office of the Tourist Information

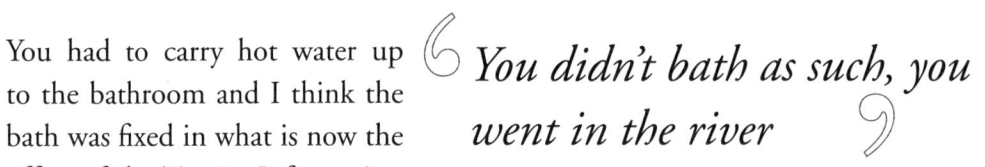

You didn't bath as such, you went in the river

[Sedbergh]. Yes, the bath was along there because there was a boiler there where you boiled water for the washing. Then you had to fish it out of the boiler, the set pot they were called. It was a fixed bath, you just ran it [the used water] away somewhere. We had an inside lavatory in the bathroom. **Freda Trott** b.1919

In 1966 I got married and we went to live in Millthrop. We 'ad the bath and a toilet. Now once a week me friend who lived just down the road used to come to borrow it, so it was bath night. We 'ad a Burco boiler, and we 'ad about that much water [three inches] in the bottom of the bath, a tin bath. And then when I'd finished we used to call 'im and 'e used to come and use it, and then 'elp us to carry it out in the street and tip it in the gutter. **John Airey** b.1942

I'd never used a bath in my life. But you had a good wash, you didn't bath as such, you went in the river in summer, and I never ever remember my father or my uncle having a bath of any kind. There was a tin bath but I never saw them use it. **Kenneth Cragg** b.1936

In 1956 I started work for Billy Hodgson [builder in Dent]. In those days he would hit it just right for the bathroom job because most people hadn't one and we would put at least ten or twelve bathrooms in round here. **Alan Mattinson** b.1934

"Our outside toilet was cold and draughty, and we often had a wind"

In the house here [Needle House, Uldale] we had taps and all that but we didn't have a flushing lavatory. We had earth closets, which was what everybody had. And we didn't have a flushing lavatory until before the war, but not all that long before, and what does rather surprise me is that none of the visitors who came to stay seemed to be surprised about this. I suppose they just thought it was the country. **Helga Frankland** b.1920

We'd all our jobs to do. Well, I know what my job was! We'd an old earth toilet wi' two holes at t' top an' that was one of my jobs. It's still standing there, sort of falling down. We'd to go out way over there. You used to have to empty it as well. They'd take it out and spread it out on the land. Yes, it was very difficult was that. We only had newspaper, all cut up into squares and put on a string. It was rather cold and was very draughty, an' it was facing the west so we often had a wind. **Betty Hartley** b.1913

I must tell you about the toilets at Garsdale Hall. You had to cross the road and go through a paddock to the toilet, it had two seats and it had a little hole in it, I think it was supposed to be a window, and we never bought toilet rolls, it was always newspapers. It was an earth closet so my dad had to clear it out every so often, with a horse and cart it would be because we had no tractors then. And my brother used to keep geese sometimes in that paddock and we were really frightened of them because they used to come hissing at us, so often when we wanted to go we had to get one of my brothers to take us to the toilet! **Mary Cowperthwaite** b.1924

Water supplies

I made a note of when piped water came to Dent – water pipes to houses about 1928. Before that all water had to be carried from the [Adam Sedgwick Memorial] fountain or from Parson's Spout, which was near the Old Parsonage, and Flintergill had its own supply. **Marjorie Middleton** b.1913

I never lived in a house with water in because when I was at Dee Cottage [Cowgill] I'd t' go up t' road an' down in t' beck an' get the water. There was a well under t' road, we got it there. We'd use mebbe a dozen buckets a day, you always seemed t' be runnin' up t' road fer a couple o' buckets!… No, no runnin' water in any house till I was in me forties. **Mary Ellison** b.1909

When we first went to Slack [Garsdale] in 1955 there was no running water, we didn't even have a sink, all the water had to be carried in and carried out again for two years maybe, and then eventually we got water laid on, and then after a while we got a bathroom and hot water, so it was marvellous. **Mary Cowperthwaite** b.1924

What we did have was jolly good drinking water because my great-grandfather and grandfather were both water analysts and they used to analyse the water round us as practice. Separately, mind you, a generation apart. They would be analysing the water for the City of Birmingham and London and different places and when my grandfather came here [Needle House, Uldale] he analysed our water. They laid on a supply to the house, and that was not what they nowadays would call potable, but there was a limestone spring not far away and that was perfectly pure water, and since one of the men had to come from Newhouse to Needle House every morning he would bring a large can of this beautiful water, which was probably better than the sort of bottled water you buy nowadays, and that went on until during the war when, unfortunately, as limestone does, this water gurgled away somewhere else and we lost it! From then on until a couple of months ago [2009] we never drank unboiled water in this house unless it was bottled water. **Helga Frankland** b.1920

"Mains water? I don't want the rubbish!"

We had a lot of problems with the water. There was a ram, which is a good thing if it works itself, but it was a Type A ram that just pumps the drinking water. For the Type B ram you had to have two supplies, a clean water supply and a supply that'll work off dirty water. The dirty water will pump the clean water if you've two supplies, which we hadn't. We've got an electric supply now, to back the ram up. **Myles Jackson** b.1928

Just to the end of the war we had to bring water in from a well. The end of the war my father put a water supply in so we just 'ad a cold tap, and one over the boiler at the side of the black range fire so all the water was boiled in there, and that was for washing the farm utensils and all our own use. **Kenneth Cragg** b.1936

When mains water was laid on for homes on the north side of Dentdale it was welcomed by most – but not all…

I don't want the rubbish! Our water [at Spice Gill, Cowgill] comes out of Jack allotments for a start, Broadmire allotments, and then it comes down through Syke Gill, comes in t' beck where I have a cistern up there. **Tom Sedgwick** b.1917

Heating the home: peat and coal

[In Grisedale] we'd just a peat fire and a boiler at the side to heat the water and an oven the other side, and me mother would bake all bread and all t' cakes we ever 'ad. Peat was one of the things that we relied upon quite a lot for our fuel. And after I got married we used to still cut peats and lead 'em in with horse and cart. **John Pratt** b.1905

When I remember them, as a boy, both farms [in Mallerstang] burnt peat, and coal I suspect was a luxury. I can remember both farms with what was called the peat house, quite a large building full of peat. **Ingram Cleasby** b.1920

"Oh yes, my grandfather knitted"

The house where I lived before I was married had peat rights going over to Ingleton, and my husband and a friend of his went up and cut some peat and left them to dry, and when they went for them somebody else had taken them! **Marjorie Middleton** b.1913

We'd coal fires and we'd a fireplace where the visitors were, in the parlour. There was a lot of stoking of the fires. And there was grates in the main two bedrooms. Whenever anybody was ill they were up there and you'd light a fire. There was a lot of work attached to being ill in those days. I was told my grandad got the coal at Dent station. They went up with horse and cart, sat on the front and knitted. Oh yes, my grandfather knitted. **Betty Hartley** b.1913

Lamps and candle light

Them days we didn't have electric, we only had oil lamps and candles, so in winter we would get up later. **Kenneth Cragg** b.1936

No, no electricity. We'd candles, and maybe a single burner paraffin lamp for your living room. But otherwise it was candles 'ere and candles there and candles everywhere! **Cissy Middleton** b.1914

All we ever had when I was brought up was candles and oil lamps. Latterly there was Aladdin lamps which had a mantle, and then it was Tilley lamps which was a big advancement on anything we had previously, but it was mostly candles. When we went to bed we took a candle to bed. **Albert Fothergill** b.1923

You could have a Tilley hanging up there and it sort of heated the place, it did. **Miley Taylor** b.1923

We [Rycrofts hardware store, Sedbergh] sold a lot of paraffin and most of my Wednesdays were taken up repairing oil lamps. There'd be a queue of a dozen or so oil lamps, Tilley lamps or Aladdin lamps, waiting to be repaired. It was a smelly job! **Tom Rycroft** b.1922

We had something that was better than an oil lamp, it worked on the acetylene and it gave quite a good light. You had to put water in one area and some sort of powder acetylene in the other and then a kind of a gas came out which you could light and it gave quite a good light, did this acetylene lamp. I wish I'd kept it because it was brass, it was a lovely thing! And then we had oil lamps as well, but to go to bed we had candles. And I used to read in bed with a candle till I heard that my father might be coming to bed and put it out quickly before he knew! **Betty Harper** b.1920

Gas

A gas company was established in Sedbergh as early as 1852 and continued to operate until it was nationalised in 1949. By 1932 it was providing street lighting for the town, and the houses on the Havera and Fairholme estates were some of the first to have gas lighting laid on.

The gas works was at the bottom of New Street, just below the Methodist chapel… There was a retort house with maybe two banks of four retorts which had to be charged up with coal, and then they would be heated up and the gas driven off, and then the red-hot coke would have to be raked out; and there were men doing this job all day in this hot atmosphere. And the gas went through various processes; it was scrubbed and had the sulphurs taken out of it… There was a big gas holder at the back of the yard backing on to Castle Lane. And there was a big stack of coke in front of the gas holder and somewhere at the side there was a pile of spent oxide that was being re-aerated…

> *A man went round lighting the gas lamps in the evening*

So a lot of people in Sedbergh had gas lighting. I remember going to get my hair cut by a man on Fairholme, and his house was lit by gas. There was always a smell and black stains on the ceiling, and sometimes a smell of sulphur if they hadn't got all the sulphur out of the gas. And I just remember, too, the gas lighting on Station Road. Of course there were no street lights during the war, the blackout period, but when the lights came back it was gas lights, mainly. And I remember all the way down Station Road, from Town End down to Guldrey, there were these gas lights, not much more than eight feet high, with a bar on the side where the gas lighter could lean his ladder so that he could get up to change the mantle or whatever. And a man went around lighting the lamps in the evening and presumably putting them out in the morning. That was before we had electric lights. **Peter Iveson** b.1938

We had a gas light in the living room which was a greenish colour and roared! **Freda Trott** b.1919

Gas lit! Go round with t' ruddy mantles. It's surprising there were no more fires, isn't it? 'Cos when you get in a proper wool place like Farfield Mill there's fluff flying everywhere. It was lit right up to [1941] by gas! **Tom Cornthwaite** b.1923

In 1955 Calor Gas came on the market so Norman [Jenny's husband] says, 'Oh, I think we'll 'ave Calor Gas light put in!'. So we 'ad Calor Gas light till the Electricity Board came round… I 'ad a gas freezer. It was handy, too, was that! **Jenny Kiddle** b.1918

Electricity

Electricity came to Dent just before the war started. The first electricity we had in Dent, Frank Dinsdale made it at Millbeck with a waterwheel, and I think that would be about 1936, but I couldn't be sure of that date. There was no generators then, Dinsdale supplied it all from Millbeck. And then later on he bought an engine, I think it would be an oil-fired engine, and I can remember he bought it from Tommy Brook at Lancaster. Supplied the whole village until the grid started. Upper dale didn't get it until the sixties. **Albert Fothergill** b.1923

My husband and I built this bungalow [Rhumes, Dent] in 1937, and we had electricity. Frank Dinsdale had his own private circuit and he supplied electricity to all Dent. It was sixpence a unit and we thought that was a lot of money in those days. You just had it for lighting, or perhaps ironing. But if you had a fire it had to be something that was just about three quarters of a watt, because it was too expensive. **Marjorie Middleton** b.1913

We had a big refrigerator in the cellar [of Dent Stores], a really old-fashioned type thing, it was built into the building and that ran on electricity. It would be one of the first things that was put in here at about 1961 when Dent basically got [national grid] electricity, 'cos down the back there they manufactured their own electricity with carboys and big batteries so they sort of ran electric round this area before it came on national grid. **Richard Goodyear** b.1944

As far as the town supply was concerned, Martins [shop in Sedbergh] had their own private power station, just at the back of the cemetery. Children were not allowed to go and play down by the power station. But when the mills at Millthrop and Farfield were taken over as engineering works during the Second World War they had to have a proper electricity supply, and Martins couldn't supply them, so Sedbergh had to come on to the national grid…

Sedbergh School used to have its own power station in the old quarry. I don't know when this was set up. It was direct current and it was generated by, I think, a gas engine, an engine that actually ran from the town gas. These engines were in use from about the 1920s onward. The school employed an electrician to run the machinery. He'd go in in the morning, start up his engine, generate some electricity – it was DC so it could be stored in a battery. And the room next to the generators was full of big lead acid accumulators that were supposed to store enough electricity to see the school through to the next day. In fact there were a lot of losses in these cables and Winder house in particular never had a very good electricity supply at the best of times. But sometimes if there hadn't been enough electricity generated and stored the lights would fade in the middle of prep, and then the boys would be sent to bed early. This was being

> *I 'ad one of the thrills of my life when I washed with an electric washer!*

phased out in the 1950s when I was in the school, and the school and the houses were being converted to the national grid AC supply. **Peter Iveson** b.1938

We made our own electricity, just for lighting [at Rash Mill, Dentdale]. In the fifties I had it put in, it cost me £60 a year for five years, that was the guarantee. And that was twelve weeks' wages then, that was, £60. They brought the line up and you can trace it right down to Barbon. They put electric into Millthrop Mill and up here at Rash, and subsequently all the farms took off it. It cost me mother ninety quid to get transformer in to get their hens lit! **Neville Balderson** b.1924

When I got married in 1957 and moved into Stonehouse [Cowgill] we had an old engine, it would only be 24-volt, the only thing it did work was light bulbs. John Blythe, he came round from Hawes and he used to have wet batteries and dry batteries, it was the wet batteries he used to collect. You'd maybe have three batteries, you'd have one on your wireless, and he'd take two and charge them up and then he'd bring them back the following week charged and take the other one, kept swapping round. **Alan Mattinson** b.1934

Electricity? Made all the difference in the world! You 'ad this light, you'd no paraffin to fill lamps, which are stinking things… and ironing, oh and washing. I 'ad one of the thrills of my life when I washed with an electric washer. **Elizabeth Middleton** b.1915

Wartime prefabs

In 1941 the Air Ministry arranged for Armstrong Siddeley Motors Ltd. to take over the old woollen mills at Farfield and Millthrop in Sedbergh and turn them over to aircraft production. This was part of a government move to relocate industries away from industrial centres which were being heavily bombed. Coventry had suffered more than most and its workers were skilled with munitions, so the government arranged for some who had lost their homes to be brought to Sedbergh to work at the mills. Sedbergh Rural District Council minutes record that in 1941 274 men were joined by their wives and children, with 'a further influx expected in the near future for Farfield, which is now working'.

Inevitably, this sudden growth in population meant that accommodation in Sedbergh was desperately short, and Armstrong Siddeley complained of exorbitant overcharging by landladies for letting apartments. The company made plans to convert existing buildings and create new estates of what the council called bungalows, but we know as prefabs.

My father got a job with Armstrong Siddeley's at Millthrop Mill. They were making parts for aircraft engines. Well, they built Pinfold and Maryfell prefabs to take the workers that were going to work in the mills, and my mother wanted to go to Pinfold 'cos they 'ad the toilets and a bath. We lived at 22, Pinfold. Well now, one concrete base holds one of those cabins. There was six children and me mother and father. And we only 'ad 'alf! Now me granny and me uncle lived at 21, so me sister, me oldest sister, moved in with me granny. Me older brother, he 'ad one room, mother and father 'ad another room, and Alan, David and myself 'ad the third room, which you could picture 'ow big it was! And then me sister was born. But Jim went into the army, so that was a bed free. And then Alan went into the army, National Service, so that bed was free. But the spirit on the Pinfold, the folk, was marvellous because they were all, like, off-comers if you will – a majority 'ad come from t' likes of Coventry. We moved from Pinfold when they built Castlehaw [1950s]. **John Airey** b.1942

I was a sub-contractor doing plumbing works and converting Settlebeck House [Sedbergh] into fifteen flats. I didn't work on the prefabs but I worked in the old vicarage and Beamsmore. They were used for accommodation for some of the bosses at Farfield when the mill was there. **Cecil Iveson** b.1907

After the war Armstrong Siddeley handed over the Maryfell and Pinfold estates to Sedbergh Rural District Council, and in 1954 the Maryfell prefabs were replaced by council houses on the same site. (We plan to cover wartime memories more fully in Volume 2).

Social housing

In 1926 a scheme was started with a view to re-housing people in Sedbergh who were living in cramped back alleys. According to a medical report of 1928 Sedbergh's yards were badly congested and all available council housing was occupied. More low-cost housing was needed but it wasn't until 1936 that the Havera estate was built, followed by Fairholme in 1939, to provide lower-income families with adequate housing. House building came to a standstill during the war, leaving an acute shortage of accommodation, even in rural areas which escaped most of the bombing. The decades after 1945 saw more council houses built, Dragon Croft estate in Dent by 1951, Castlehaw and Langstaffe in Sedbergh in the mid-fifties, and Castlegarth, Sedbergh in the mid-sixties.

My father lost all of his stables with the building of Havera on Howgill Lane. He just had the stable for the horse, the cow, the calves, the pig, because we always had a pig. The Farrers, who had the coal cart, they were the first ones to lose because Fairholme was built on part of their land. Masons, they lost their land.

During the war their land was taken over and they built prefabs for the workers from Coventry to live there and to work at the Farfield Mill and Millthrop Mill and Birks Mill. **David Hutchinson** b.1920

Pioneering sheltered housing in Sedbergh

We moved onto Havera, which was a council estate of thirty-six houses, and everybody knew everybody else. I remember on the day we went to see the lady whose house we were taking over, me sister, who was about four at the time, was intrigued by the flush toilet because we didn't have any flush toilets at Firbank, we just had one of those earth toilets outside. And the lady said, 'Does she have something wrong with 'er bladder, because she's constantly been in the toilet?'. And me mother says, 'No, she's just sort of overwhelmed by this flushing thing', she'd never seen anything like it before! **Shirley Tebay** b.1947

Havera initially was built for the less favoured people in Sedbergh that weren't as well off as others and that was all supposed to be low-cost housing. I think most of them paid their rent but they were people that couldn't afford big money. But I can't think there'll be much poverty in Sedbergh now to what there was then. **Leslie Robinson** b.1930

Sheltered housing

The post-war Labour Government recognised the need for social care, especially for the elderly. Mary Gladstone's father was a leading figure in Sedbergh in the 1950s and a social pioneer.

He had been quite a name in the town when he was at the prep school at Settlebeck, and when he retired everyone pounced on him – 'You can do this, you can do that'. So he became a churchwarden at St. Andrews, he was already a lay reader. He became chairman of the local council, when there was a Sedbergh Parish Council. He was also chairman of the Magistrates' bench when Sedbergh had its own. And during his time the plans for Gladstone House and sheltered housing were put into practice, one of the very first places, I think, certainly in the north, to have sheltered housing with a resident warden. Unfortunately he died just before they opened Gladstone House and they called it Gladstone House in his memory, which was lovely. He was a very practical, no-nonsense person and I remember him often saying 'Oh, I could have knocked their heads together, make them see sense!'… Sheltered housing now is generally accepted. But this, I think, was one of the very first. **Mary Gladstone** b.1926

Offcomers – the new property owners

In the seventies there was work, 'cos all these grants were flying about for converting old houses, modernising them, and there was a 75 per cent grant from the government to improve these houses. There was a lot of work about, and it did well for a lot of people. **Billy Milburn** b.1938

I probably came in close to the beginning of the arrival of so-called offcomers, not at the very beginning by any means but I certainly notice a lot of people coming into the valley since I came and I would say that the age group of the people that have come in has changed as well. I remember thinking when I came here, there were an awful lot of retired teachers, professionals, and that's changed quite a bit now, I think there are younger people who can work from home or are prepared to travel more. If the house prices keep going up then young people won't be able to afford them. I mean, young indigenous people can't afford to live here, full stop. So if the house prices keep going the way they are, it's only people who are wealthy and retired or very well-off professionals who are going to be coming here. **Chris Payne** b.1959

CHAPTER 10

Love and friendship

Courting – Marriage and honeymoon –
Looking after each other –
When it went wrong – All sorts

There are some things no-one ever forgets: courting, marriage, honeymoon… and the old traditions of neighbourliness and looking out for each other.

Courting

We went for tea and I can remember William sitting opposite me and looking across at me, and he winked at me, and I think that was it really. He can still turn me knees to jelly when he gives me that wink! He proposed to me the second time he took me out, I was nineteen and I said 'Oh, I can't get married till I'm twenty one', and we did get married when I was twenty one. **Mary Airey** b.1945

Mary and George Ellison were interviewed together.

Mary: His friend started courting my friend, didn't he? So of course I went out wi' George. I went with him for nearly six year so I really knew 'im. I was only seventeen.

George: It was at a Chapel harvest sale up at Cowgill, that was in September. When she come out I said, 'Well I'm going to walk you home'. We came right over Ewegales bridge and right down by Nelly bridge and that's how far I took her home. That was the first time. And I was doing this for five and a half year… Aye well, it was worth it. She was worth waiting for.

Mary: Well I couldn't leave grandma you see. I was just fifteen [when I went to Dee Cottage] but I had been sleeping there for over a year to see that they were all right. They were both getting old and it was a natural thing to do in those days… He just cem up t' t' 'ouse, we didn't do nothing! We 'ad a shop yer see, an' one of us 'ad t' stop in t' look after it, an' we'd just be in t' house, that's all! **Mary Ellison** b.1909 and **George Ellison** b.1908

❛ *I didn't want to be teed up by t' neck when I was 17* ❜

I met Betty Oversby from Grayrigg at a dance at the Masonic Hall in Sedbergh. I walked out with her and in those days we only had push bikes and I'd to push bike to the top of Firbank to near Grayrigg to do me courting. It would only be Saturday nights to start with and probably Sunday nights. I never had much time anyway, it was all work and bed really. **Albert Fothergill** b.1923

Me dad only lived at Garsdale Hall. An' he always said he got t' first woman he came past, 'cos this [No. 1, North View] was t' fust house after his house! He didn't look about! **Mary Allen** b.1923

I didn't start till I was twenty five, I didn't want to be teed up by t' neck when I was seventeen! He 'ad a bicycle, it's only means that he could come, and 'e 'ad t' bike all t' way from 'ere [Selside] to Dent. Went together five year, we did, an' I was four years older than 'im. **Bessie Mason** b.1911

There used to be a gentleman called Walter, he used to have a big blue van an' he used to sell fruit and veg an' he'd come all the way from Kendal, an' Tom, my future husband, would come over in the van and just sent a note out with Walter which was passed to me, an' things just developed from there really. Yeah, we used to do our courting on a big fruit and vegetable van! We used to go up Dent to one of the pubs for scampi and chips in a basket, then we'd come back home in the early hours of the morning. You could always tell when I was coming home 'cos it was a noisy van! **Judith Allison** b.1954

Marriage and honeymoon

Mary: We married in Cowgill Church, so they charged George a bit extra, didn't they?
George: If I'd lived in Cowgill it'd only been seven and six you see. Well he had to read t' banns out at Dent, so it cost two shilling a Sunday for three Sundays. And then there was a shilling for t' marriage lines.
Mary: We had it on a Thursday because it was closing day. People hadn't enough money in those days to be running their parents to expense like that. We med our own wedding breakfast and we just asked t' nearest relations, didn't we? We'd have offended people if we'd gone any further. We cooked two legs o' lamb and a lump o' beef… We got over a hundred

They had to repair to the White Hart to get over the price of the bouquet!

wedding presents! Everybody brought wedding presents. Even people I'd never have dreamt would have brought something! **Mary Ellison** b.1909 and **George Ellison** b.1908

We'd been up at t' Congregational harvest, and that was t' first time he brought me home… We went for three years and we got married on November 25th, 1939. I provided more or less all for me own reception. There was a friend made me cake and there was a lady in Dent made me some vanilla slices, and I think Metcalfes at Sedbergh provided me wi' t' cups and saucers and glasses, whatever I needed. But you see we would have a few hams of me own, of our own killing, so me dad gave me about half a pig to start me in me house. And I remember getting a huge piece of beef – it was cooked in t' washing boiler! **Cissy Middleton** b.1914

I was married at Garsdale Church, June 21st 1945. We had a reception at home because there was rationing then, and we just had the two families and a few friends… I had a white dress made and the flowers were red carnations which my father got from Stephensons at Sedbergh. He was so appalled at the price of flowers that they had to repair to the White Hart to get over the price of the bouquet! My sister was bridesmaid, just one, our Rose, she was about twelve then and my husband's brother was best man. He was on leave from the forces, luckily, because we hadn't known till the last minute whether he was going to make it, but he did. **Betty Harper** b.1920

We got married on Boxing Day 1940, Dent Church. We did quite well. I wore white satin and paid for [the dresses] myself, mine only cost three pounds seven shillings. I bought it in Kendal and we got the three bridesmaids' there as well, they had red sashes and white dresses. And it was a glorious day, the sun shone from morning to night! **Betty Hartley** b.1913

> *Someone wrote on the car 'Going to Morecambe for a little sun and air'*

It was a job to get coupons for you to get your dress and I went to Lancaster and got a dress for four pound summat. I still 'ave it – and it 'ad a train and I didn't want a train so I chopped it off! **Bessie Mason** b.1911

Well I know that morning I was scrubbing the kitchen floor and Billy Bracken came by and he said, 'You shouldn't be doing that on your wedding morning, somebody else should be doing it'. I said, 'It has to be done!'. **Mary Cowperthwaite** b.1924

I went for me 'oneymoon t' Littleborough… she was aunt to me 'usband or else I don't think we'd a hed an 'oneymoon. We went on t' train, [for] a week. **Bessie Mason** b.1911

We went to Lytham 'cos I had an uncle at Lytham. We went to stay wi' them for a week. **Mary Allen** b.1923

Roger and the lads took me and Tom to Morecambe for our honeymoon and someone wrote on the car 'Going to Morecambe for a little sun and air' – but the son and heir didn't come till 1954!… Just one week, we went into a bed and breakfast place and Tom's dad paid for it, we hadn't hardly any money at all really. **Mary Cowperthwaite** b.1924

We got no 'oneymoon; it was straight into work. Straight out o' work, and straight into work! **Cissy Middleton** b.1914

We went to the Isle of Man, '67. The only thing I remember, we stopped at the Sefton Hotel in Douglas and the first person I met, he said to me 'Are you on honeymoon?' and we said 'Yes'. He said 'I thought so, your shoes are so clean'. Oh dear! So we got caught out straight away 'cos in those days we hadn't the wherewithal or anything… caught out first morning! **Richard Goodyear** b.1944

They eloped to the Sportsman's Inn just like they go to Gretna Green

Mary: [My son Bob] was born the end of January in '35. I was in bed a month at home and then in hospital ten week so I didn't see Bob much till he was a big lad.
George: There was a lot to look after him. They were all coming running! Teking him walks all over, we'd lose 'im all afternoon, 'e'd be round Dent town. There was a Mrs Thompson, she come for him; there was two young women next door, Miss Foxall and her friend. They

were always teking this blue-eyed baby boy out. And then he had his two aunties, Renee and Elsie. **Mary Ellison** b.1909 and **George Ellison** b.1908

When it went wrong

[I married] first time in 1948. My wife eventually went off with [another man] soon after I took over the shop. I remarried eventually, but divorce was looked down on altogether. Things were totally different then to what they are now. **David Hutchinson** b.1920

My first marriage was a failure. A lot of it was me own fault because when the children were born I never had any time for them, I was too busy working. **Albert Fothergill** b.1923

There was an elopement in Dent. They got on t' train at Dent station and went to Liverpool and they never caught 'em. And then there was another elopement, and they eloped to Cow Dub [Sportsmans Inn, Cowgill] like they go to Gretna Green. Aye, all sorts goes on!… They say once a hoss 'as bolted it'll bolt again, an' that's what me brother Jack used to say about marriages. Once a wife 'as bolted she'll bolt again! Loose living! You see, if a wife 'ad gone off for 'er 'olidays or summat, they'd put t' brush out o' t' door, 'cos if they put t' brush out o' t' door a woman would come along an' visit 'em!… It was a saying, 'Have you got t' brush out o' t' door?'. But it would go on, wouldn't it! **Bessie Mason** b.1911

Courting, marriage and raising a family was, then as always, the bedrock of life in the community. But the community was bigger than the family. It extended to friends, neighbours, and anyone and everyone who might need a helping hand.

Looking after each other

Well it was a strange way but a wonderful way. You didn't go and help deliberately but if one of your neighbours had a problem – for example one of our neighbours once broke a leg – nobody said anything, you just went an' took your horses an' did his jobs for him till 'e got better. Nobody ever thought of paying one another, there was no money changed hands, and that particular man I'll never forget.

Years and years after I went to help him my father wasn't so well and I was doing all the jobs on my own, an' he turned up one day an' 'e was spreading manure in our field, an' he'd just come an' done it and there was nowt – there wasn't even a thank you, he just did it, and we knew why. Anyone else wouldn't understand why, but we all knew, an' this is what was done. You used to help one another.
Kenneth Cragg b.1936

Garsdale was a great community, a lot of people wouldn't have as good parents as we had neighbours… At one time you had to double dip your sheep, there must have been scab on, and the police used to come, they'd be having a great day out because they had their meals with us and I can always remember we were sat having tea and mother putting some of the currant bannock out and this policeman had some. I could tell by the look of him that he was having a good time. He ate that and then he said 'Would you mind if I had another?'. That well pleased my mother. **Dick Harrison** b.1934

An aunt of mine was the district nurse and she had a caring attitude towards her patients. It was an understood thing and it made for a great happiness in the community, and security too. Old people were cared for, very often in their own homes, until they died… Yes, a wonderful spirit was abroad. Anyone who was short of food due to illness and father not being able to work, good neighbours made sure they had plenty to eat and the children were cared for. It was like a miniature welfare state but not organised by any central authority. **Jack Dawson** b.1922

We'd a very good chap lived at Netley Pot [Gawthrop]. He was a farmer, Tom Park. And he was an amateur vet, but he was good. And everybody seemed to go to him. And he used to say that there was a root or a flower or a fruit or a herb that would cure all animals' ills. And he found out a lot of 'em. The snag was when he died he had never told anybody. But he was a marvellous chap and he was just an ordinary farmer. I don't know [where he learned it]. Just knocking around. Aye, 'e saved many an animal after the vet said 'Get the knackerman in'. He used to be out at all times of the night and he said, 'I'll tell you what: folk talks about this, that and t' other, but I never saw anything any worse than meself at night!'. **Willie Whitwell** b.1914

[The neighbours] got on alright with me. Well, it was down in me contract! Me deeds of contract! That I 'adn't t' fall out with anybody. So I was over a barrel. But it's the worst thing yer can do is t' fall out with neighbours. Yer bend over backwards t' keep reet o' 'em. Eat 'umble pie fer a certain amount of time but say what yer got t' say eventually – but yer don't do it too soon! **Reg Charnley** b.1942

I think it was better in t' old days like, you knew everybody an' they were all kind o' honest. Thou could leave thy coat down at roadside and they wouldn't tek money out o' pocket. Take bread out o' thee mouth now, like! **Tom Sedgwick** b.1917

❝People are described as having a lot of work in them, meaning they've never done much❞

The Sun Inn [Dent] was where all the old farmers went and the George and Dragon was where all the youngsters went and never the twain did meet. But on Christmas Day Bill Mulliner, who then owned the George and Dragon, used to put a free buffet on and we used to do one [at the Sun] on Boxing Day, so then the embargo between pubs went out the window because people then got two free meals! New Year's Eves were always very good… Every single person came out and they went round peoples' houses at twelve o' clock, which doesn't happen now 'cos there isn't that many in the village that are actually occupied! But yeah, it was fantastic, and there was always the ones who you may not have seen for six months, but they were always welcome for a drink on Christmas Eve and New Year's Eve. Yeah, it was a very good community. **Eddie Smith** b.1949

[As a policeman] I often dealt with sudden deaths in the Sedbergh area. They were very, very personal but because I knew the individuals and the family, and they knew me, we could relate to each other and I always feel, you know, it was part of a police officer's duty… I felt that the people could cry on my shoulder and I could comfort them without any problems at all and we could break down that barrier of emotion, which a stranger can't do. **Dennis Whicker** b.1951

There's a great deal of care goes on. There's a lot of what would be seen from the outsiders as just busy-bodying, people being nosy and a lot of people say 'Oh, we haven't seen you around much this week', but underlying that they often mean 'Are you alright? Is there a problem? Have you been ill, we haven't seen you around'. And it's partly the language that people use round here as well. Nobody would ever say 'Oh, we haven't seen you, have you maybe been ill this week' or 'Have you not got any work?' or whatever. They would just say it in a very English, modest, understated way… People are described as having a lot of work left in them, which means they've never done very much, they've been very economical, worked very efficiently through all their lives and not over exerted. And if you ask people how they are, they are either 'gay wonderful', 'fair to middling' or whatever. I remember once asking a chap how he was and he said 'Send for Bruno!', Bruno's the local undertaker which meant that he wasn't feeling up to scratch that day…

People tell me they used to come in here [Dent smithy] when Billy Hodgson's father was here, Old Willan, and they used to pump the bellows for him after school, and they all say he used to say they were the best bellows pumper going, which kinda tells you that Old Willan was quite a wily character 'cos there was no point in telling a kid he wasn't very good, he'd probably go home, but if you told him he was the best one he'd come back the next day! They pumped the bellows for years and years until the electric came, and probably longer still 'cos he was tight enough not to spend his money and keep the kids pumping the bellows. I don't think he ever parted with a penny – maybe gave them a sweet or let them hold a horse! No, I think the idea was you paid him! You came along with your horse after school and asked him to shoe the horse and he'd get you to pump the bellows and do all the work. **Chris Payne** b.1959

Everybody knew me before I knew them and there was that respect between the police and the community at that time, and I found that a little bit difficult to comprehend because there'd been so much animosity elsewhere, but in Sedbergh they were very law-abiding and I found that looking at the police officers who've worked Sedbergh in the past, most of them were community orientated so it made my job very, very easy in coming and dropping in really. There was never any real crime at the time and occasionally people would just sort of step off the line so you just sort of edged them back on again and that was good fun to do and you earned their respect…

One good example, there was one particular farmer, he used to ride around in a battered red van and I didn't know him at the time and I saw that he had a back light out. I stopped him and I said 'I just want to explain to you that you have a defect on your vehicle' and his reply was 'Nay lad, you must be the new copper!'. So we just had a laugh and he knew all about me but I knew nothing about him so he had me at a disadvantage, but eventually I got over to him, I said 'You've got a defect on your vehicle' and he said 'Nay lad, have a toffee!' 'cos he always kept a bag of toffees on the dashboard, so I'd a toffee with him and off he went. And I thought, well, I'll probably be seeing him later on and giving him another talking to, but the next day it was fixed. **Dennis Whicker** b.1951

There were two banks in Dent, only part time by this time, and I dunno which year it was but we were going past in one of our minibuses and the alarm was going off like mad. So we screeched to a halt, piled out, rushed into the bank ready to bash an intruder, and there was nobody there! He says 'It's alright, it's alright, we were just testing and it's been going off for an hour and nobody's taken any notice. Thank you, thank you for taking some notice of our alarm!'. **Ben Lyon** b.1939

All sorts

I remember Clockie, we used to call him – I think his real name was Parrington. But he used to mend clocks so he got the name Clockie. He lived at High Chapel [Dent] and he was a dwarf, really, and his legs were crippled and he had really long hair, but he was quite a gifted man. And he was a member of the church choir and quite a good tenor… Somebody took me over to his place to see him when I was a little girl and I was really quite scared of him, 'cos he was so different to anybody I'd seen before. **Betty Hartley** b.1913

The gypsies used to come once a year, great excitement, the children used to run down to the street to watch… most beautiful caravans, beautiful horses. Then the women used to come round to all the doors and sell pegs and everybody was terrified of them! My mother, when she died, she must have had hundreds and hundreds of pegs. But they were beautiful pegs, made of English oak. Dolly pegs. Fortunately I had saved some and I made both my girls dollies and I dressed them. That was the thing about the gypsies – everybody was very frightened of them, that they would put a curse on the house. But they told fortunes and some of those things, of course, came true! Another set of people who came, who must have been pre-war, were the onion sellers from France. They tended to walk. Coming all that way! But those were gorgeous, those onions, plaited, weren't they? Beautiful! I remember those! We had those hanging in the kitchen. **Jean Rochford** b.*c*1927

CHAPTER 11

Church and Chapel

Church – Chapel – Sunday school –
Closures – Cradle and grave

As in most rural areas, church and chapel played a major part in the life of our local communities. There were the parish churches in Sedbergh and Dent, both dedicated to St Andrew, and the outlying C of E churches in Cowgill and Garsdale, both named for St John. But the Nonconformist tradition was strong, represented by churches and chapels scattered across the dales. Sedbergh had its Methodist and Congregational churches, the latter now United Reform. Dent had no fewer than five Methodist chapels: the Wesleyan in Laning on the site of an old Quaker meeting house, the Primitive Methodist almost opposite at Meadowside, and three outlying chapels at Dent Foot, Deepdale Foot and Cowgill. Dent also had the Independent or Congregational Zion Chapel in Flintergill, now the Dent Meditation Centre. Garsdale, Grisedale and other scattered communities had their own churches and chapels. Quakers, once numerous in the area where the Society of Friends originated, continued to meet at the old Brigflatts meeting house, and occasionally at Lea Yeat where regular meetings ceased in 1911 but which continued to be used for special occasions.

Here our interviewees recall both the religious demands and the social delights of church and chapel life which marked their journey from the cradle to the grave.

Church

Well, I've been belonging t' church [St Andrews, Dent] since I was eight year old. I was in t' church choir then, and I've been a part of t' church ever since. There would be at least thirty [in the choir]. Men's stalls used to be always full, and then three up one side and two rows on the other of ladies. Oh yes, we'd a good choir. And it used to be t' schoolmaster that took it, you know, conducted and trained us. We used to sing anthems at special occasions, Harvest and Easter, we'd allus have anthems then, and t' vicar used to come down out of t' vestry and out at the back door, and the choir would walk round and come in at t' porch and sing from there… Of course in those days we used to have Evensong at Wednesday night as well, and Litany every third Sunday. And you got Choral Communion first Sunday in t' month, it was all sung in those days… I remember once, I went without a hat, and I was sent out because I hadn't a hat on me head. Housekeeper at t' vicarage then, she wouldn't allow me into t' church because I hadn't a hat on. And this was for a choir practice! **Cissy Middleton** b.1914

I'd been brought up [in Sedbergh] as an Anglican and hadn't really met anybody from other denominations, so [when I went to Cambridge] it was a great eye opener that there were Christians in other denominations as well! [When I moved to London] we used to sing the Messiah in its entirety, starting at half past two we sang parts 1 and 2 and then there was a long interval and people would go out into Kensington Gardens and picnic, have their tea – I always associate it with hot cross buns and Lyons cup cakes – and then we would go back into the hall to do part 3. So that was something to remember and rejoice in… We came back [to Sedbergh] in '86, me and my brother, but there were still people around who remembered us as children, and a lot more who remembered our parents, of course, from the fifties! So we knew a lot of faces. But we were welcomed back, and I remember the first time we went back into St. Andrews Church, where we were both baptised, the person on sides duty, a newer person to Sedbergh, said 'Welcome to St. Andrews', so we wanted to say, 'Well, no! We belong here anyway!'. It was the place to come back to, the home town, the home church. **Mary Gladstone** b.1926

…no 'anky panky or t' vicar would have looked down his nose at us

Being a member of the Church of England in the 1940s meant going to Sunday school twice on Sunday in the National School building. So we went to the morning Sunday school at about ten o'clock, and just before half past ten when the matins started we trooped together up to the church and we sat at the back near the belfry. And we had to be silent; a word out of place and you got a clip behind your ear from the teacher who was sitting behind you. I remember at that time the middle part of the church being almost full, and even some people sitting in the transept at the side. Then there was Sunday school again in the afternoon, and then church again for Evensong in the evening. And again Evensong was well attended. **Peter Iveson** b.1938

Sunday was a rest day. We 'adn't t' work on Sunday, only jus' what was necessary.

Mother wouldn't allow that. Sunday was t' be Sunday an' she would see that we got t' church, an' we were given strict instructions there was t' be no 'anky panky an' we 'ad t' behave ourselves or t' vicar would 'ave looked down 'is nose at us!… We allus 'ad t' walk down t' church every Sunday morning, four or five of us, an' it was mind yer behave yerselves, there's no giggling and laughin' an' any talkin' in church, yer 'd got t' be quiet an', yer know, they were really strict with us about that. And then we would come back, 'ave our dinner and we would march off to Sunday school, in t' day school. And then when we were in t' choir we'd to be at Sunday night as well, as long as we'd somebody to bring us home… Yes, very happy days. **Cissy Middleton** b.1914

My grandparents certainly were strict. My parents were a little more tolerant but my mother tells a story of my grandparents coming home from church one Sunday night and finding us playing tiddlywinks, and thought that was disgraceful! That was terrible! It's hardly work, is it, tiddlywinks? **Tom Rycroft** b.1922

Sunday roast – on the best crockery

Sunday was always a roast, either roast beef, lamb or a chicken. Never a lot, but always some sort of a roast for the full family, that was the one meal mum always insisted everybody had together. **Judith Allison** b.1954

Sunday was always different with us. The Sunday tea was different and the crockery and everything, everything was different. We'd all our best china and everything like that and me mother's grandfather's sugar basin, and lump sugar! **Elizabeth Middleton** b.1915

There were feast days, and sale-of-work days…

I remember the Harvest Festivals. We went to Frostrow and all the children carried little baskets of fruit. We'd a lady on Bainbridge Road who used to make them for us. The boys would take something like a marrow or a cabbage or something of that sort, and then on the Monday night there would be the auction sale of harvest gifts and all the farm lads from round about used to bid against one another to see who could buy the most fruit and veg. **Isobel German** b.1925

[Easter and Whit church sales] were different in those days to what they are today when most of the things have been manufactured stuff. In those days it was all what people made, like pegged rugs, knitting, there was always cakes – it was a sale of work and you had Cissy Middleton down at Gawthrop, I always remember she used to bring her plants and other sorts of things, she was a baker, and then there was Nancy Murdoch who really was on top of the game, ordering everybody about – but you have to have somebody like that, no good faffing about! I remember taking some cakes and we said £3.50 or whatever. She said 'You silly boys, £5!'. She made the money, you know! **Richard Goodyear** b.1944

…and 'the playing of the merry organ, sweet singing in the choir'

I played [the organ] for me first service when I was fifteen. Me stepmother was t' organist and of course she sort o' showed me how to play it and what stops I'd to put out, 'cos I hadn't had a lot o' tutoring in music, but I could just sort of read it, and I would learn, and I would work 'ard… An' so of course when they came t' be without, in 1947 I think it was, there was no organist available, I said, 'Well, I'll come an' see what I can do!', an' so I went down an' I played for fourteen years. There was two services as a rule. Sometimes if there was a children's service I would do three, and eight o' clock Communion on special Sundays. **Cissy Middleton** b.1914

> *We'd all those hanging oil lamps to fill and clean*

I joined Dent church choir when I was ten… Yes, there was some farming folk but there were a lot of the in-comed people you see now. And we had a King's Messenger branch, it was to do with the church, but we had all kinds of demonstrations on crafts and people to talk to us, and it was really quite social. **Betty Hartley** b.1913

… and lots of opportunities for voluntary service.

Since 1937 I've been one of the twenty-four sidesmen at the church in Dent. I think it'll be a record [58 years]! Me father was one. Me grandfather wasn't but me great-grandfather was. They didn't just take anybody, you had to have your qualifications! **George Ellison** b.1908

We always kept the church clean, caretakers of the church for years up t' dale [St Johns, Cowgill]. We kept the fires going, had to light 'em on a Saturday and then go in Saturday night to stoke up, all to do, all three. And we'd all those hanging oil lamps to fill and clean. I used to polish all those seats. It did seem to tek a long while when you were by yourself, you know, we spent hours polishing them all. Yes, we cleaned all t' church. We just did it ourselves, nobody else did it. I used to like cleaning the brass against the organ, but to try and get t' floor clean, there was no Hoovers, no nothing. Carpets took a lot o' keeping clean… I used to scrub that war memorial to try and keep it clean. I knew when they put it there 'cos grandad gave t' marble for it and they'd med a cross. And it came back rough round t' edge. Oh, grandad was disappointed, I can still see him. He said, 'They should have polished it all, then we could hev kept it cleaner'. I kept that clean; I know all the names. **Mary Ellison** b.1909

‘The only time I saw my father in church was in his box at his funeral!’

We had a big exhibition in the church when we were celebrating Adam Sedgwick, who is the most famous son of Dent, being a professor of geology at Cambridge. [In 1985] we were celebrating the two hundredth anniversary of his birth, an exhibition with all kinds of valuable things. Cambridge even sent us the little bag and hammer that he used to go round the dale with when he was a boy, getting little bits off various stones. We had to take great care of these valuable things. I know we slept in the church in turns, to look after them, mainly two ladies at a time if they couldn't get their husbands or sons to stay with them. I don't know what we would have done if a burglar had got in, but we were there, to keep guard over them! **Betty Hartley** b.1913

But then, as now, church life didn't suit everyone.

My mother, she never went to church, only on special occasions – Easter Monday and Whitsuntide and Christmas and those times. Me father, the only time I saw me father in Dent church was in his box on his funeral day! **Albert Fothergill** b.1923

When I went in the army my boss said to me (he'd been in the First World War), he says, 'Don't be Church of England. You can be what you like, but don't be Church of England'. I said 'Why not?'. 'Well', he said, 'they have a Church of England parade every Sunday but the others don't!'. So I put me religion down as Methodist. The sergeant-major used to say 'Church of England stand over there. All you other fancy things, dismiss!', so we had the Sunday morning off. The Church of England were marched down to the local church. And 'You other fancy religions', he used to say, 'dismiss'! **Willie Whitwell** b.1914

Chapel

Methodism followed on as successor to Quakerism in the Dales and to some extent in Sedbergh. Then Quakerism gradually faded out, as it wasn't quite so evangelical as the Methodist Church, so the Methodists moved in, I think from the Kendal direction, and there was a kind of rash of chapels built in various valleys leading out of Sedbergh, Cautley, Garsdale, Dent. **Jack Dawson** b.1922

> *At Quaker meeting we used to sit on a form, and nivver nowt 'appened*

The Quaker meetin'… [Lea Yeat meeting house, Cowgill]. My friend from church, Mrs Bannister, she used t' say 'Come with us t' Quaker meeting'. 'Well', I says, 'I'm playin' at chapel that day'. 'Well', she says, 'I think they'll not want you that day'. Anyway, I got in touch with the other organist and she did the service for me at the chapel while I went t' the Quaker do. Well you know what it is, the Quakers, you jus' sit an' wait an' sit an' wait an' sit an' wait, yer don't know when they're goin' t' start! Anyway, I was twiddlin' me thumbs, I thought, well, I wonder when are we goin' t' start? I wished I'd 'ad me organ in that back room, I'll tell you! I could 'ave been playin' some tunes! **Jenny Kiddle** b.1918

A meeting was held once a year [at Lea Yeat] to keep it in the hands of the Quakers, and me mother used to take us and we used to sit on a form, and nivver nowt

'appened. Me mother thought it should be still kept open, an' it was a good thing because they had that place for funeral teas, for the church funerals as well. At the meetings, quite nice gatherings, nobody never said anything for a long, long time, then somebody got up and spoke. I should be about eleven or twelve. I remember it closing. It became a Reading Room I think [Cowgill Institute] at t' front, and t' little room was at t' back for the Quakers. It was a gathering place for everyone.
Bessie Mason b.1911

All the social life in the dale was based on chapels or the Church, but for us it was the chapel. Actually the local [Methodist] chapel was in our field… and the main events of the year were the chapel tea parties, when there was a special service and a meal afterwards. How the ladies of the chapel managed it, I don't know! I remember my mother going to chapel to do what she called 'cutting up', that was preparing sandwiches, perhaps, and cake, and then there would be somebody to provide tea, too, which wasn't easy when there was no electricity. **Betty Harper** b.1920

When we were young your whole life was centred around a cluster of people at the chapel. Deepdale chapel was almost our second home… we used to have a potato pie supper in February for the Christian Endeavour. Then we used to have the Sunday school anniversary the first weekend in September, a supper and an entertainment. Then the first Sunday in December we used to have the chapel anniversary and a supper. We always had suppers, in the school room. And we had four tables on trestles and we would probably have two sittings down. We had cakes, always plenty of cakes! Then you would have a choir, perhaps Beckfoot Choir or Garsdale Gospel Singers. **Elizabeth Middleton** b.1915

You went every Sunday but there was do's on Saturday nights, tea parties as we called 'em, an' I used to help and other girls did

> *We even went to prayer meetings to have a night out*

as well, at supper time. You see, younger folk came, they gathered up when there was a supper, an' I suppose lads came as well to see what was going on and see who was there, so that's how you met up with other young folk, really. It's how I did! The chapel was really the main thing that was going on then, you see, we went to them all, whatever. If there was a special do on we would go to Hawes Junction on our bikes and then if there was one at Garsdale Street we would be there, or Garsdale Foot. **Mary Allen** b.1923

We always went to chapel every Sunday and then on Sunday night there used to be a lot of boys and a lot of girls and we used to walk, the boys behind the girls, down the middle of the road, there was hardly any traffic at all. It was mostly things to do with the chapel, we even went to prayer meetings to have a night out, just as an excuse. We were strictly brought up, we weren't allowed to be out when it was half past nine. **Mary Cowperthwaite** b.1924

Methodists didn't seem any different to me. I think they were all teetotallers, yes. I think we all were in those days. It was the war that got us into pubs. **Marjorie Middleton** b.1913

We went to the Band of Hope, the one my mam went to in the Congregational church [Sedbergh] and it was run by a Mrs Douglas. I was about seven or eight. They would talk about not starting to take strong drink, and you signed the pledge. I signed the pledge at about nine years old and I've kept it as well. **David Hutchinson** b.1920

My grandparents belonged to the Methodists. I used to come to the little old Methodist chapel here in Millthrop with my grandfather when I was a kid. But my mother and father were Congregationalists and I went to the Congregational Sunday school every Sunday. A lady called Mrs Douglas used to take us, and a Mrs Potter, she was one of the teachers as well. Yeah, there was quite an attendance there. **Billy Milburn** b.1938

[Sedbergh Methodist] was a very flourishing church and it also had quite an active life outside Sundays. There was a Guild, a very flourishing Guild in those days. I should think there would be fifty, sixty people, fourteen years old and upwards, who used to go on a Monday night, and then on Tuesday night there was a Junior Guild, and we had a Guild song and we used to have a little service and a speaker and play games afterwards. **George Handley** b.1937

Sometimes there would be very, very special occasions at the chapel when there would be somebody called an evangelist who would come for what was called a Revival, which was sort of to bring people into the chapel who maybe hadn't been before or who had stopped going. In a Revival, with a special preacher, the audiences would be very large, everybody would go for every night for the week, perhaps, and then things would calm down and people would gradually go back to what was happening before. **Betty Harper** b.1920

"...a Garsdale preacher of a fierysome kind, much taken with damnation"

The big occasion of all the year was the Camp Meeting, on the first Sunday in July it used to always be. The preacher would stand in a horse and cart and preach from the cart in the afternoon. Then in the evening they went inside for what they called a Love Feast. They came round with biscuits and water, and then anybody could talk a little bit about their Christian experiences. **John Pratt** b.1905

In Dent there was a Wesleyan chapel and also a Primitive Methodist chapel where Meadowside is now. It's got 'PM' in the cobbles outside the door. Deepdale was also Primitive Methodist and Millthrop was Primitive Methodist, and Cotterdale and Hawes Junction, and I think Garsdale Street. We got each others' preachers. And then it all changed, we all united as Methodists [in 1932]. **Elizabeth Middleton** b.1915

John Willie was a local [Garsdale] preacher of a very fierysome kind. He had red hair and he was much taken with damnation. **Ingram Cleasby** b.1920

We went to [Beckfoot chapel], all four of us. Yes, I've preached there, and at Sedbergh, Tebay, Staveley, Crook, Kendal, Whinfell. Me mother wanted me to be a Methodist parson. There was four of us. The other three stuck to it – they were the Reverend so-and-so. I kicked out for some reason, fell by the wayside. **Willie Whitwell** b.1914

I was invited by Miss MacKenzie, the organist of the Congregational Church

[Zion Chapel] in Flintergill, an' I used t' play fer 'er whilst she was on 'oliday. It's a beautiful organ. **Jenny Kiddle** b.1918

Me father was a farmer and a local preacher. I think he was, though I never heard him actually preach. I think he was a reasonable lively preacher by what people tell me, he'd bring dialect into it, and farming. Yeah, he lived a lot for his preaching. **Myles Jackson** b.1928

> *It was a matter of 'were you saved?' and 'Hallelujah'*

Father, he was a local preacher at Deepdale chapel, he used to go to Garsdale, Grisedale, and everywhere. He didn't qualify – I don't know there was any qualification at all, was there? I've heard him preaching a sermon in the barn – there was nobody there, just to nobody. We did occasionally have family prayers and you were expected to say your prayers before you went to bed… I rebelled. They had revival meetings a lot, you know, they used to get a bit carried away. I was a teenager then. When these revival meetings came you were expected to go three times a day. Well, I just couldn't. I used to see people get up and say this and that and I thought, bloody hypocrites! It was always a matter of 'were you saved?' and they'd sing 'Hallelujah!', you know, they got carried away! **Miley Taylor** b.1923

Sunday school

The big event of the school year when I was at Garsdale school was St. John's Day when we were taken to St John's Church for a service, but the important thing was that in the afternoon all the children went to the vicarage for tea on the vicarage lawn. Nobody stayed away from school that day! You put your best clothes on of course! We had to tolerate going to church in the morning but it was worth it for the tea. And the Sunday school trip was one of the highlights of the year. We were taken in a charabanc, an early form of coach, which would pick us up and take us to Morecambe. What a thrill! Everybody was looking for the first sight of the sea! It was a wonderful day out. We used to play on the sand, have a donkey ride, the dodgems. **Betty Harper** b.1920

They started a Sunday school when I was about seven or eight, something like that, there was that many children in Grisedale then. **John Pratt** b.1905

We always went to the Congregational church at Flintergill [Dent] every Sunday morning, and we went to Sunday school in the afternoon where the superintendent talked, we held prayers, and we sang. And then we had a wonderful Sunday school party at Christmas. **Marjorie Middleton** b.1913

They used t' have a Cautley Picnic, an' it was Frostrow, Cautley an' Fell End chapels, all the scholars… We ran races an' we got a free tea an' a free supper. **Eva Middleton** b.1923

Sunday school treats were a great thing. We didn't get many treats in the 1940s. I mean, even going up to Lily Mere for a picnic was a treat – it was the big event of the year to look forward to. Once I got to Queen Elizabeth Grammar School one of my best friends in my class was George Handley, from a prominent Methodist family. George introduced me to a lady on Back Lane [Sedbergh] called Mrs Harrison who used to run evangelical meetings for boys. Mrs Harrison had lots of exciting toys for boys to play with. There was Meccano and train sets and these toys were not common in the 1940s. And after we'd played with these toys for half an hour she called us together and she had a Mr van Doran from Capernwray Hall who conducted a sort of evangelical prayer meeting, singing choruses and that sort of thing. And the great treat if you went to these meetings was a trip to Capernwray Hall in the summer, near Carnforth, which was an evangelical Christian centre. It was like a Sunday School treat. Anyway, through George I sometimes went to the Methodist Junior Guild too, but my family were Church of England and so my experiences were mainly with the church… After we got too old for the Sunday school there used to be a Bible Class. At that point they separated the boys from the girls. There was boys' Bible Class which the curate took, and the girls' took place somewhere else. I remember going up on to Bainbridge Road where the curate – I think it was Ambrose Southward, who became Rural Dean of Windermere. We must have been about fourteen years old then and it was a more formal Bible study than what we had done in the Sunday school. **Peter Iveson** b.1938

Another event in the [Methodist] chapel was the Anniversary when you would say a poem. You'd be given a religious recitation to say – quite an ordeal. And it probably wouldn't be a poem of your own choosing, it was what you were given. And of course there was the prize-giving at Sunday school as well, and depending on the number of attendances you had you were told how much you could spend on the book for a Sunday school prize. There was a catalogue came round with all the prices and the names of the books, and you were told how much you could spend, depending on how often you had attended. So of course, when it got near the time for Sunday school prizes you would go every time! **Betty Harper** b.1920

Well, of course I went to Sunday school and as I got older I was roped in to being a teacher with little ones. I'd sang in the choir with Bert Trotter as the organist, then Bobby Woodhouse got me into bell ringing [in St. Andrews, Sedbergh]. **Jean Rochford** b.*c*1927

When I was at school I had to go to church every Sunday three times and I hated it! And if I played truant and didn't go, I got a good hiding when me mother found out. And when I left school I thought, well, I would never go to church again, I was so fed up with going to church… and then when I joined the army it all started again with church parades, and I hated it! **Albert Fothergill** b.1923

Oh yes, we went to church, C of E, but to the Congregational as well occasionally. My grandmother was very religious but I don't think my father ever did. I think he'd been forced to go so much when he was a child that he rather rebelled. **Neville Balderston** b.1924

My wife came that much, she used to do Sunday morning, Sunday school and evening time 'cos her father was, in those days he was law and she had to go three times a day. So now she says 'I'm not going near the damned place', and she doesn't. But she did go on Easter Sunday with me and somebody said, laughing, 'What're you doing here?'. **Richard Goodyear** b.1944

Closures

Most people in Grisedale went to chapel at that time. But the chapel was sold off

The chapel people 'ave left and people are getting old

after. It closed and was sold off and is now a house. **John Pratt** b.1905

I remember going into Grisedale once just for a ride out and we overtook Mrs Allan going back to the chapel. They'd had the final service there a few days before, and she was going to collect their own personal hymn books. We picked her up and gave her a lift and we went into the chapel and dad went up into the pulpit (he'd preached there many times in the past) and my mother and Mrs Allan were sat in the seats. I took a photograph just as a record of what it used to be like. We didn't know that it had actually closed down but it's just one of those things. These dales get depopulated and it's a case of having to close down some time. **Isobel German** b.1925

[I was a member of Deepdale chapel] 'til it closed. It was the end of an era, the end of a lifespan that we'd known. We came out triumphant, victorious, I said we're not coming out defeated! It was in a way forced upon us because if you come as low as five members, which we did, and they'd spent all this money on re-roofing it and refurbishing it, they 'ad to go under Sedbergh, and then this last few years I don't think really that anything much 'ad been done at these chapels and it's like these farmhouses, we've come to the time when they all want doing up y' see, putting bathrooms in, re-roofing… I think really the chapel people 'ave left and people are getting old. So we said we'd join Dent and they closed Deepdale and it made £20,000. **Elizabeth Middleton** b.1915

Oh, I've sung at all these little chapels, Grisedale, Cotterdale… The minister used to take us and it used to be dark and I used to have to get out and help him with these gates. I never knew where I was until we got a car a good few years ago, and I hadn't a clue where I'd been. I remember when we were at Cotterdale the last time they were converting the chapel into a house and there was the poor old harmonium outside. I said to a friend, 'Gosh, I've sung to that old thing many a time!'. **Doris Waller** b.*c*1920

It's a pity it's gone, but life's changed dramatically, hasn't it? Bingo started, didn't it, and people going to the pub, you know, which they've every right to do. The discipline at school went for one thing and so I think the Sunday schools died out when the discipline stopped because when we were at school you never ever answered the teacher back, you just didn't. It was unheard of and I think that's why the Sunday schools went. It's a pity. I can only say that it was good. I enjoyed it. **Billy Milburn** b.1938

There's quite as much religion and dedicated Christians today, but there's the television. A lot of people tell me they love the services on the television. There's good singing and everything. Yes, it provides an alternative to worshipping, 'cos everybody can't go to God's house; they're not well, or old… all kinds of things can prevent them. **Elizabeth Middleton** b.1915

Oh well, we 'ad a lovely farm'ouse kitchen an' all round t' sides was done wi' old oak from out of [Dent] church. Well, when they did away with a lot of box pews in t' centre of church, we must 'ave bought a lot of this old wood an' it was all panelled, all round, oh, as 'igh as this mantelpiece, jus' a bit 'igher, with this lovely oak. **Cissy Middleton** b.1914

Cradle and grave

I went to Dent for [the christening of daughter] Christine. Me mother would look after me and Christine was born in t' living room at Backstonegill [Dent]. Thistlethwaite was t' doctor then… An' me 'usband didn't turn up [at the christening] because t' clocks were put back or forrad, I don't know which, and he misfired you see, he didn't come. **Bessie Mason** b.1911

Although my grandfather was a small farmer here he was also the local registrar for births and deaths. In Dent, in this very house [Mill Dam, Gawthrop] there was a notice on the porch at the front where it said 'Registrar for Births and Deaths'. Well my grandfather died in 1927 and my father would take it on until about 1947 I think, when it was all done from Sedbergh… My move into funerals was slow. I had to do mundane jobs, which

> *You'd see some fancy gowns which they'd prepared for their own death*

was sanding coffins and polishing and things like that. In those days they were nearly all elm coffins, and by then you used to buy coffins in a set, they were really like flat-pack, and a good man could make a coffin in a day, and then polish it and seal it round with pitch, round the inside to make sure nothing ever run out of it, because you've got to remember there was no chapels of rest in those days. They stayed at home, it could be three days, four days…

Most coffins were left open, people would go visiting but it wasn't a social occasion I don't think. Most of the old folk used to have their own burial clothes, they used to make them, a gown, and knit their own socks to be buried in. It was one of the things they thought about. You used to see some quite fancy gowns which they'd prepared for their own death. There was a horse-drawn hearse which was kept in Dent and sadly it was sold for £45. Dent used to hire that hearse to Sedbergh. I've seen it recorded what they used to pay, and they would come up from Sedbergh and they would take the horse and hearse to be used there. David Rowe was the last person to do this, I would say it would be just before the war… I can remember before I left school there was a taxi firm in Dent, they had an Austin 16 car, and they used to take the back seat out and they could slide a coffin in. And that was the hearse. I can remember being quite fascinated by seeing this car going past with a coffin stuck out at the back! After that you could hire a hearse from Kendal, but in Sedbergh, for most of them out of the town we had a wheeled trolley, a hand trolley, which we used to wheel from the church right down to the cemetery and back again. **Brian Goad** b.1942

My dad had a joiner's shop, where you turn up to Cowgill Grange, a building on the other side of the road [later Ben Munroe's bike shop, now demolished to make way for the Cowgill Community Orchard] – well he had that as a workshop 'cos he had all t' coffins to make, he did all funerals. He did it all by hand, he just had to saw and hammer. Timber, he used to fell it a lot himself. He'd go up at Carla [Carley Hill, Cowgill], up at back of there there was a paddock and it was full of fir trees and we felled all those and took 'em all down to chop, cut 'em all up into field lengths, length of a rake head, and took 'em down to workshop. **Mary Ellison** b.1909

My father [Bert Hutchinson] would come from Sedbergh station to Harvey

Askew's shop at the town end and Mrs Askew would ask him if he was going to a funeral up Garsdale, and if he said yes she'd say 'Well I would like to go with you'. So she would get on to the front of the hearse with him and off they would go up Garsdale. In the course of the journey he would ask her if she knew who the person was whose funeral they were going to and she'd say 'No, but it's a nice day today for a ride out with you, and you get a tea at the end of it and a ride back home!'. **David Hutchinson** b.1920

> *Before we got to the committal, water was lifting and the coffin was coming up and turning over!*

It would be 95 per cent burials when I started. I can remember very few cremations in the fifties but there would be some. Dent people were buried in Dent churchyard or Dent Methodist churchyard or the United Reformed, and Cowgill would be buried in Cowgill churchyard. Sedbergh churchyard closed about 1878 and that's when the cemetery was opened, bearing in mind that that churchyard, like Dent, had been buried on for a thousand years. So it was quite normal if you were digging in the old part of the churchyard you would come across the remains of somebody that had gone before. It's like the Quaker burial ground at Brigflatts, I mean there'll be nine hundred people in there and it's not much bigger than a hundred square yards, is it?… In Dent churchyard they always had a sexton who rung the bells and dug the graves. I've dug them myself, I've dug graves for £5, thinking I was well-paid. But the ground varies, doesn't it? I mean look at Cowgill, you wouldn't be paid fairly if you got £300, would you? It's that rocky and stony, terrible! And at Dent it can be worse because it fills up with water. I can remember when someone died and they were ladling the grave out until we got to the grave-side, and we put the coffin in and before we got to the committal water was lifting and the coffin was coming up and turning over! It 'ad to be covered up as you're not allowed to take a coffin out, are you? **Brian Goad** b.1942

I don't know whether we're supposed to say this on tape, but Bob Udale pulls up one day. 'Come on,' he says to Billy, 'we're going to Northallerton to pick the Reverend B up'. They git to Northallerton and they pull this body out of t' morgue and were going to load it up when Billy says 'Nay!' he says, 'it's t' wrong fella!'. Bob said 'It's a good job I fetched thee!'. It was, wasn't it? **Dick Harrison** b.1934

CHAPTER 12

Fun and games

Dancing – Entertaining ourselves –
All the fun of the fair

*L*ife in these dales could be unrelenting, but people played hard too. They clearly knew how to enjoy themselves before the arrival of television and mass entertainment. In this final chapter of Volume 1 they recall the dances, games, 'sittings', and home entertainments where musical talent flourished, and the great annual events such as Dent Fair which bound the community together and punctuated the routine of daily life. 'Aye, there was some good do's then!'

Dancing

Oh yes, we had some good enjoyment wi' dancing yer know. 'T isn't like t' rubbish they do now! We had Lancers and t' Cottages an' Paul Jones, Eva's Two Step, in fact I do a bit of Eva's Two Step now if I can! **Bessie Mason** b.1911

We had dances in Cowgill school, it were sixpence fer a dance an' a shilling fer yer supper. We did two steps and three steps an' everything. An' when we got up into our teens we all got together at 'ome an' me and me pal we learned all t' lads t' dance. They wanted t' go t' dances but they couldn't dance! So they came in an' we used to side [clear] all away in t' house, an' we had thick lino down an' we put gramophone on or played t' piana an' learned them all the steps. We learned 'em t' waltz first because if yer could waltz, you could do any of the others… We used to have some nice dance dresses. I had one, a blue one, oh I did like it, long one, satin it was with a little silver top to it, oh I thought it was smart! Seventeen! **Mary Ellison** b.1909

[At Cowgill school] we used t' 'ave Mr Beresford's Band from Hawes. Now 'e was very noted. It was always 'Beresford Band will 'ave t' come, we'll 'ave Beresford Band fer dance'. They 'ad the drummer, they 'ad the guitar an' one o' these 'ad a piano accordion. Oh we 'ad t' 'ave a trumpet, it wasn't complete without a trumpet! They played dance music – ballroom dancin'. There were some jolly good dancers in Cowgill in my time, I'll tell yer! They were allus up, there weren't many o' 'em sittin'! If there wasn't anything goin' on in Cowgill we used t' go down t' the Dent do's. **Jenny Kiddle** b.1918

There was a postman over at Ingleton, Mr Newbold, and he'd bike over and he'd play on t' piano, he'd play for a dance all night. Well, usually after a whist drive he'd come and he'd play into the early hours of the morning fer ten shillings. But we wanted him to play on if there was a good do, we went round wi' hat for him. And t' odd tuppences and thrupences amounted to a lot more than what his ten bob was, so he'd play well while three or four o'clock in t' morning. He got on his bike and he had to bike to Ingleton and had to start posting at half past six. **Mary Ellison** b.1909

There was a dance every week at Dent. We used to go on t' bike; there was no cars. I used to put me bike in t' smiddy. They were at t' school, in t' Memorial Hall. There used to be a band come from Bentham and there would be a piano player and accordion. And they would play while about one o'clock, and then they'd be having sich a good do they would go round wi' t' hat… Aye, there was some good do's then! And there was nobody fresh o' drink, neither! No, they didn't get to t' pub, they went straight to t' do. **Jim Middleton** b.1913

We used t' 'ave sixpenny hops an' you would go down t' Dent and if they 'adn't a proper band this 'Pop John' would come an' play. 'E allus wore a green sort of neb [peaked] cap, it looked as though it was green with old age! 'E 'ad a fiddle an' 'e would stand in t' middle o' t' room an' 'e would throw 'is hat down an' 'e would dance round 'is hat! Well he would get over that an' then 'e would play fer everybody else t' dance. **Cissy Middleton** b.1914

> *Visiting other houses for all the local gossip, that's how people caught up with the news*

Sometimes there were concerts up there [Tank House, Garsdale] and sometimes they used to have a dance after. I remember one time I thought 'I'm going to stop at the dance', and I did. I stayed and was dancing and the next thing I knew dad was at the door, 'Where's our Mary? Come home at once!'. So I had to get on my bike and pedal home and I got a really good telling off from mum and dad! **Mary Cowperthwaite** b.1924

When we had a do there [Lunds] all the people used to come with their Tilley lamps, they'd no electric. It was a real sort of little gathering of locals. And there was some nights we'd play away until there was only two or three Tilley lamps, people 'ad been going home and took t' lamp with 'em! **Garth Steadman** b.1945

Entertaining ourselves

'Going a sitting', making music, and billiards in the Dent and Cowgill Reading Rooms helped fill the after-work hours.

We used to visit other farms and other houses, that was part of your entertainment, visiting other people. We used to tell ghost stories and all sorts of weird things, and all the local gossip. That's how people caught up with the news. **Betty Hartley** b.1913

We would start about Christmas time, and you'd go a sitting to one another's houses. You know, somebody from Gawthrop 'd come to visit somebody up in Deepdale and mek it annual do's. They'd come and they'd stop while three or four or five o'clock in t' morning. That was going a sitting. Just talking away, like. And then there's a few 'd have napping parties. Played nothing else but nap all night, some of 'em. If they wanted a bit more sophisticated and let t' women people in, they'd have a little whist drive in t' houses. We had a lot [to do] in wartime to raise money. **George Ellison** b.1908

An old chap, 'e used t' come every Saturday night from Bower Bank [Gawthrop], 'e was Teddy Capstick an' 'e used play 'is melodeon to us. Every Saturday night some of us would be getting bathed in front o' fire, kiddies an' all, but 'e would play 'is accordion. It was like our entertainment but 'e come a-sitting, you see… Me an' me sister we used to pop upstairs and there was a big, long passage an' we used t' dance to [the accordion], we used t' learn t' dance. They little knew! **Cissy Middleton** b.1914

One of the regrets I've had in me life, I should 'ave 'ad piano lessons an' I didn't because they said if thou goes thou's a sissy! The girls had to play the piano an' I wish I'd gone. But I could play the piano accordion by ear, an' the mouth organ, of course… Med your own music, aye. It often 'appened there was a bit of a sing-song [in Dent Reading Room] an' it wasn't caused by alcohol because we weren't drinking alcohol t' do it, we jus' enjoyed singing. **Miley Taylor** b.1923

Mrs Willan lived at t' Hill House [Dent], they had a farm. And in our teens we used to all go there [to do concerts], and she learned 'em. We were short o' men, lads wouldn't join in up t' dale, they were very shy, but two or three from Dent came up. I wouldn't go on t' stage, which we put up in the end of the school, but I pulled t' curtain and prompted. **Mary Ellison** b.1909

'We'd no money to go to pubs or anything'

My wife was a very good whist player and she took me along to play whist one Friday in t' Memorial Hall [Dent]. I'd never played whist in my life, and we got so many black looks and people twittering about me because I played the wrong cards, so after that I never went again. I used to go to domino drives 'cos I could follow spots, but I wasn't very good at that either. **Richard Goodyear** b.1944

I got involved with the shoot. Joe Ogilvy was the gamekeeper an' he asked me if I would run the beaters, so I did, I run the beaters fer about ten years. An' it was great fun fetchin' all t' young lads from down Sedbergh area who used t' come beatin' an' I 'ad t' keep 'em reet, I have a foghorn of a voice on t' fell an' I used t' keep 'em reet. They would give me a tot of whisky or whatever was going an' that was it but it was good days out on the shoot! Marvellous! Meetin' a different category o' folk, but they were lovely folk. We did have a social time when we got back to the Sportsman's Inn. I remember once 'aving t' be carried 'ome, loaded up into t' back of a Morris 1000 pickup. I'd been singing, I'd been drinking whisky and Drambuie and God knows what. **Reg Charnley** b.1942

The New Year was a great event because first of all there was a rugby match where the ones that have done well at school [Sedbergh School] took on the ones that had left and come back, so it was the Old Boys against the present ones. And then at night there was a Father Time party and it was four families got together, Hutchinsons, the Sloanes, the Halls and the Potters, and you each invited a friend to a party but they had to pay in order to come, the money provided for the food and the hall and everything else, and there was usually some singing and dancing. Miss Wreay, she would do a play. There was a wonderful feast and just before midnight they kicked the old year out, and when the clock struck then in came Father Time and welcomed in the New Year. **David Hutchinson** b.1920

We went to the [Dent] Reading Room to play billiards. That was the only social life. We'd no money to go to pubs or anything. **Albert Fothergill** b.1923

Cowgill Reading Room I used to go to, oh aye, and there was quite a lot round t' fire. There were billiards, reading t' papers. There was books and magazines and that. **Jim Middleton** b.1913

I loved reading, I'd read anywhere! Grandma wouldn't let me have a light upstairs 'cause she only had candles and lamps, so once flashlights came out, when anybody brought a battery back an' changed it in t' shop, I'd get that battery an' it generally did me a night under t' bedclothes t' read a book! Everything that I could get 'old of!... [As an adult] I was a member of the Cowgill Institute and the womenfolk who were members could go there. There was two coal men at the station an' one of those 'ad a paper round and 'e 'ad a motorbike and he came down an' brought all the papers, came on train an' put 'em in the Reading Room an' then people went and collected them. We allus got Daily Express and Yorkshire Post, Daily Mail, the daily paper every day, and two or three weekly papers, Woman's World and Home Notes, anything! We were all fond o' reading! And there was a library in the Reading Room but it was getting very old-fashioned and tattered so they brought the County Library in, three big boxes kept coming every month. And different folk looked after it, and opened it every week. **Mary Ellison** b.1909

We'd put earphones on, an' that was first wireless I ever heard

Beyond the bottom of Joss Lane [Sedbergh] there was Clarks' lending library. Before we had this public library, which was free, there was this little shop that made a living by lending books out to people for a penny a week. I think he also sold gramophone records and a few toys; it was a very small shop run by two elderly people. **Peter Iveson** b.1938

The cinema, black and white and silent till the talkies came, was a big attraction, and radio was increasingly popular. Television arrived in the fifties, but few homes could afford a set.

I can remember 1926 when t' strike was on. I was going t' school then. Our 'ead teacher, 'e was in t' old vicarage, an' 'e took us round t' listen to a wireless, and we'd t' put earphones on, an' that was first wireless that I'd ever heard. **Cissy Middleton** b.1914

The cinema was at the town end [Sedbergh]. It was quite a big place and it was run by a Mr Beswick, but the man who did the operating was a Mr Clark. His wife, Mrs Clark, she was in front of the house and she kept you in order and you often got a clip on the ears if you didn't behave yourself, and one of their sons did the operating. They were silent films in those days and Audrey Milburn was the pianist, and in the exciting times when the chase was on then the music became louder and louder and later on it cooled down a little bit so the playing got less and less, and that was quite an amusing time. Thru'pence was for children and you sort of sat in the front of the place, the prices rose the further back you got, so if you were in the back seat of course you spent a lot of money just to sit with a girl at the back seat. **David Hutchinson** b.1920

Madge Hancock was one of the first people I remember in Sedbergh to have television, she had it before we did and I used to go down there on a Saturday night with her permission to watch television, just for the sake of watching television, black and white of course! **George Handley** b.1937

Television has had a big influence on family life I think, and far too many children watching television. Of course, we'd no television and to listen to the radio was our highlight. **Tom Rycroft** b.1922

❛Trotting, galloping, hobby horses, all at Dent Fair❜

All the fun of the fair

I can remember when Dent Fair came, where t' car park is now, that used t' be a field right up t' roadside. There used to be these stalls and there would be donkeys on t' roadside. They would tek yer down as far as Hippins fer a ride. There were swing boats an' hoopla an' roundabouts. **Cissy Middleton** b.1914

They used to 'ave a brass band, and this man used to speak off a flat wagon and get people to sign t' [teetotal] pledge, but me father wouldn't let us. We 'adn't to do it, 'e thowt we should 'ave a strong enough mind to resist it. Because if you signed t' pledge and you broke it you were worse than ivver. And then they would set off playing, and children following t' band up Flintergill and around. And then they gathered together in that field, Jackie Holme, and 'ad sports. **Bessie Mason** b.1911

For Dent Sports they used t' get Kirkby Lonsdale Brass Band an' I think the Band of Hope as well. They used t' start at fountain an' come up town, go up Flintergill an' right round, an' all us children would follow it. Then they would walk down on t' field where t' sports were, an' they would play, an' they were champion! **Cissy Middleton** b.1914

Trotting was once a year, it was at Dent Fair and people used to come from all over just for the day. A lot, thirty could trot, good racing. We had coconut shies and things, there was the fell race up Rise Hill. You could see them going up and back again. **Betty Hartley** b.1913

All my young life Dent Fair was Saturday after Whit Saturday. Relatives who had been brought up in the dale and had moved off always came back to Dent Fair, always. It had the sports, foot running and fell running and trotting and galloping. But originally when I was very young, about the time I started school aged three or five, there used to be hobby horses and things like that, and some of these events were held at Stone Close which is now the car park. It was a very big event all my young life, was Dent Fair, right up till after the war. **Albert Fothergill** b.1923.

...and there's more to come. Telling It Like it Was, Volume 2, will mine our archive for further memories of the changes local folk lived through in the earlier twentieth century. We aim to look at shops and shopping, motor vehicles and the transport revolution, local trades, businesses and mills, and wartime as experienced by local people at home and abroad. Many of those who contributed to this book will have more to say in the second volume, where they will be joined by new voices on new subjects. Volume 2 will also include a full index covering both volumes. We plan to publish it in 2017.